£9.95

# Tread Lightly Here

First published by
The Window Press
Trowels, Pound Street
Petworth, West Sussex
1990

© PETER JERROME AND JONATHAN NEWDICK

Designed by Jonathan Newdick

Typeset in Garamond No 3
by Dorchester Typesetting Ltd.,
Dorchester, Dorset
Printed and bound by
Biddles Ltd., Guildford, Surrey

ISBN 0 9504830 1 X

# Tread Lightly Here

An affectionate look at Petworth's ancient streets

## Peter Jerrome

> Petworth has a proud history and knows it.
> Almost the visitor can hear the whisper from
> those old Georgian houses, "Tread lightly here;
> This is a hallowed place".... The very air is
> heavy with memories.
>
> "BGH" in *Southern Weekly News*, April 1935

The Window Press
1990

## CONTENTS

|  | Introduction | 7 |
|---|---|---|
| 1 | North Street | 11 |
| 2 | Church Street | 25 |
| 3 | Park Road | 37 |
| 4 | Lombard Street | 43 |
| 5 | East Street | 55 |
| 6 | Bartons Lane | 79 |
| 7 | Angel Street | 89 |
| 8 | New Street | 103 |
| 9 | Middle Street | 113 |
| 10 | Grove Street | 123 |
| 11 | High Street | 133 |
| 12 | Golden Square | 149 |
| 13 | Market Square | 165 |
| 14 | Saddlers Row | 201 |
| 15 | Pound Street | 207 |
| 16 | Station Road | 219 |

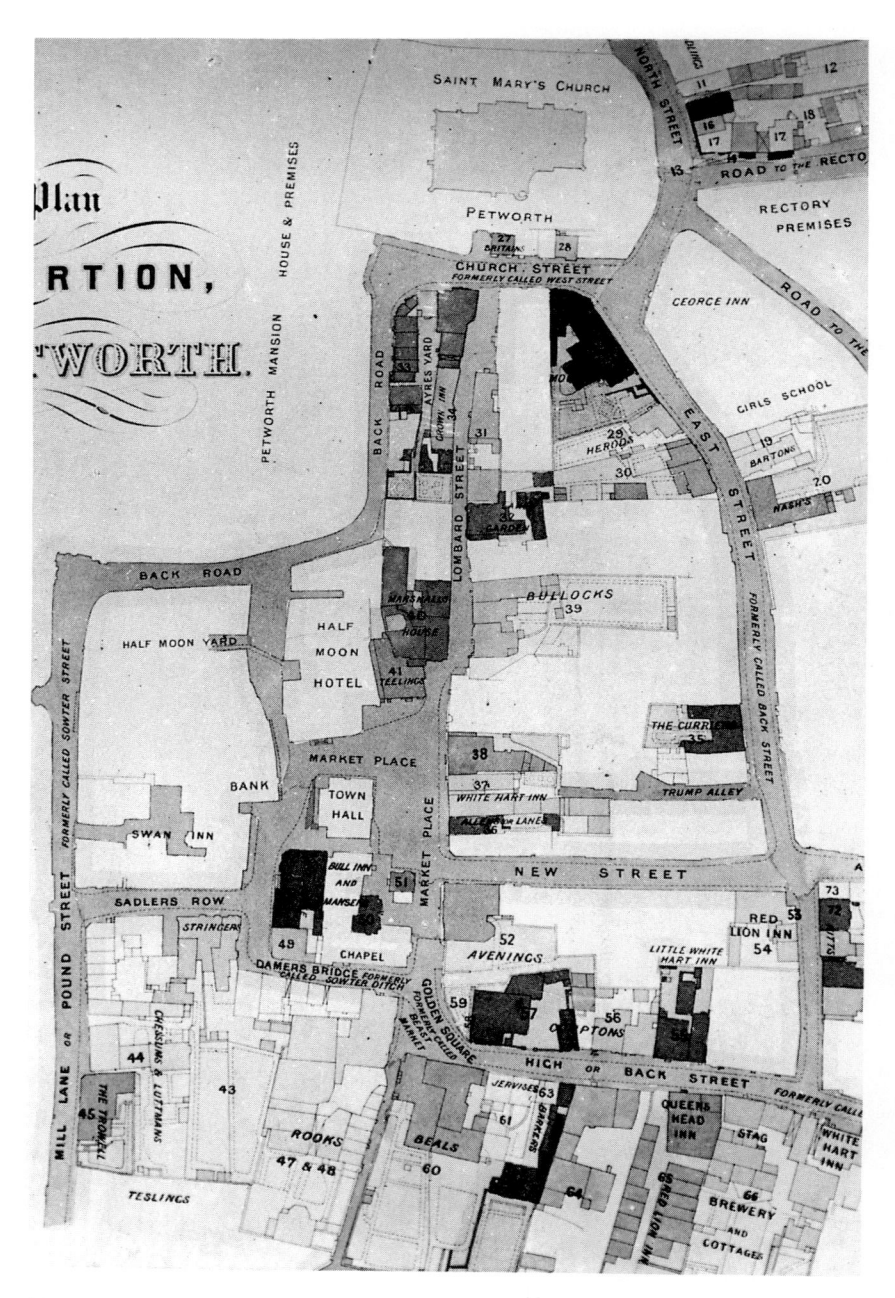

The central portion of the 1882 Survey map. Older names in italic capitals. The map appears very reliable. It is reproduced here by courtesy of Lord Egremont. *Petworth House Archives.*

# INTRODUCTION

THIS book deals with the sixteen older Petworth streets, their history and their traditions. It does not deal with St. Mary's Church or Petworth House, both of which already have competent accounts written of them, nor does it mention West Street except in passing. The sixteen streets are all part of modern Petworth as they were once of an older Petworth. Much, I am sure, might be added by a few hours judiciously employed at the West Sussex Record office, much too by communing further with older inhabitants, but this book is large enough already. There can hardly be a definitive book on a subject as diverse as Petworth's streets and these pages make no claim to provide one: any historical journey around Petworth's ancient streets will stop, start, linger or pass on at the whim of the writer. Certainly there are a few things that any writer must mention but there are a myriad others that depend on what knowledge he has to hand, or quite simply on what interests him. I would hope only that this book will encourage further discussion and enquiry and that its inevitable errors and omissions will stimulate more than they irritate.

In reviewing a wide sweep of history I have taken the turn of the present century as a convenient focal point and travelled backward and forward at will. The turn of the century stands now at the extreme limit of oral recall and in retrospect looks the Golden Age of Petworth as a small country town. I have reproduced in full a series of descriptions of local businesses that appear in *Views and Reviews*, effectively an early kind of advertising brochure produced by W. T. Pike and Co. of Grand Parade Brighton in 1893. While allowance needs to be made for a certain excess of zeal on the copywriter's part, the details given are of great interest. I have tended to take little account of post-war Petworth: the nearer one gets to the present day the more uneasy the perspective. I have included modern trade and house names more as pointers than for their own sake.

Sources are usually indicated in the text but some of the more enduring may be mentioned here. First and foremost is the actual recollection of Petworth people as preserved in the quarterly Bulletin or Magazine of the Petworth Society, the two titles having come of late years to be effectively interchangeable. Without the tradition thus preserved such an enterprise as this would have been vastly more difficult, perhaps even out of the question. Sometimes I have simply used detached recollections but more often I have quoted directly and, in some cases, at length. John Osborn Greenfield, whose *Tales of Old Petworth* written in the 1860s was annotated by a friend some thirty years later for publication in the Horsham-based *West Sussex Times and Sussex Standard*, has been a presiding spirit while any writer on Petworth must retain an awareness of the meticulous standards set by the Rev. F. H. Arnold in *Petworth: its History and Antiquities* (1864). Much has come to light since Arnold wrote but no one has ever written of the town with such accuracy and incisiveness. Miss G. M. A. Beck's short article *Some Petworth Inns and Alehouses* in SAC 99 is a model of its kind, while I have found G. H. Kenyon's famous study of Petworth trade inventories useful on several occasions (SAC 96, 98, 99). Lord Leconfield's *Petworth Manor in the Seventeenth Century* (1954) I have used from time to time but its basic strength lies in its treatment of the outlying copyholds which fall outside the scope of this book. I occasionally refer to *Petworth and its Surroundings* by Mrs. L. C. Barnes, No. 26 in the *Homeland Handbooks* series and published in 1902. Within its limited scope this is a most competent work and still of value.

I owe, as one would expect, a considerable debt to the Petworth House Archives. Individual documents are mentioned in the text but the great surveys are referred to throughout the book. Appropriately enough the 1882 Estate Survey map forms the frontispiece of this book: it is an invaluable guide to ancient place names, the annotator clearly having access to information not obviously available to us. PHA 3955 with which the 1882 map is directly related is in part an abstract of entries from the Petworth House Court Books made to accompany the 1882 survey. I quote frequently from this, occasionally too from the Survey of 1575 and Crow's great Survey of 1779. Ralph Treswell's Estate Map of 1610 marks of course a cardinal point in any history. I have touched very lightly on the Petworth House Deeds. Their extensive use would simply have made this a different book altogether. I would judge that detailed advances in our knowledge of Petworth's historic streets will come in large measure from this quarter. I am grateful to Lord Egremont for permission to reproduce material from Petworth House Archives and I am grateful also to Mr. J. E. Taylor of the Leconfield Estate for so much help over many years.

First and foremost among documents not connected with Petworth House is Public Record Office SC6/Hen 8/3481 PFF 3447. This is one of a series of annual account rolls submitted by John Ederton, collector of rents for Henry VIII, and reflects a time when the Percy family fortunes were at a low ebb and the Manor in the hands of the king. This particular roll comes from 1541 and is of the greatest importance for Petworth's older streets. I am grateful to Mrs. Alison McCann, archivist at Petworth House for her rendering of the difficult Latin hand into English, as over the years for so much other advice and assistance.

The Petworth census records from 1841 to 1881 are the backbone of any study of Victorian Petworth as too are the Directories, Kelly's over the years but also odd issues like Pigot's for 1826 or Bennett's for 1899. Reference is sometimes made in the text to the minute book of the Church Vestry Committee, a lineal ancestor of the present Parish Council. The years covered are 1804 to 1830. A short typescript prepared in the late 1940s by Dr. J. M. Brydone is a valuable source of oral traditions that have not otherwise come down to us. Invaluable too is material preserved in the Oglethorpe and Anderson collection of solicitors' material at the West Sussex Record Office and I make reference to this from time to time. Occasionally too I quote from two handwritten books of recollections set down in 1966 by the late Edwin Saunders of Station Road.

Photographs come in large measure from the work of Walter Kevis and George Garland as preserved in the Garland Collection in the care of the West Sussex Record Office but I have not hesitated to go outside that tradition when I needed to. As so often I am grateful to John Mason for his crisp and sensitive printing from glass plate negative. The reader will find many pictures of an older Petworth in *Petworth Time Out of Mind* (Window Press 1982). I would also like to thank Mrs. Janet Austin for the account of Otways in Chapter 13 and Mrs. P. Watson for her skilful typing of my manuscript.

PETER JERROME<br>
PETWORTH<br>
MAY 1990

Abbreviations

ARNOLD: HISTORY   The Rev. F. H. Arnold: *Petworth: Its History and Antiquities*, 1864.
BARNES   Mrs L. C. Barnes *Petworth and its Surroundings*. (The Homeland Handbooks No. 26). 1902-3.
BECK: INNS   G. M. A. Beck: *Some Petworth Inns and Alehouses*. Article in SAC 99.
CCP   Peter Jerrome: *Cloakbag and Common Purse: enclosure and copyhold in sixteenth century Petworth*. 1979.
CVB   Petworth Churchwardens' Vestry Book 1804-1830.
KENYON: TOWN AND TRADES   G. H. Kenyon: *Petworth Town and Trades*. 1610-1760. (SAC 96, 98, 99).
LECONFIELD   Lord Leconfield. *Petworth Manor in the Seventeenth Century*. 1954.
NAIRN   Chapter on Petworth by Ian Nairn in Nairn and Pevsner's: *The Buildings of England: Sussex*. 1965.
O&A   Oglethorpe and Anderson material (mainly at West Sussex Record Office).
PHA   Petworth House Archives.
SAC   Sussex Archaelogical Collections.
TALES   John Osborn Greenfield: *Tales of old Petworth*. Reprinted 1976.
WSRO   West Sussex Record Office.

# 1

## NORTH STREET

IN EARLIER days North Street was not usually, as it is now, a visitor's first impression of Petworth. Instead, alighting from the train at the station, the visitor would approach Petworth from the south, the horsedrawn station bus clattering up the long incline from the mill to the bend at Stoney Hill to glimpse a town spread out, as it seemed, beneath St. Mary's tapering spire. In the age of the private car however, North Street is most often the visitor's first and abiding view. In high summer particularly it can be austere and almost claustrophobic; unwelcoming certainly. The high wall on the right bears in on the traveller while, at the same time, acting as a screen on which the sun throws the shadows of the chimney stacks. The cars parked on the left hand side enforce a certain circumspection. Through the ribbon of houses that hugs the road on the left hand can be seen tantalising glimpses of unattainable open country. No doubt for many, as they pass through, this claustrophobic impression never leaves them. When they eventually attain the crown of the hill they grind with what speed they may through the narrow streets to reach once more the haven of open country. If Petworth is really the feudal outpost that outsiders claim it to be, then North Street with its high wall is at first sight an initiation into that far-off world. Pedantic perhaps to point out that, so far from being "feudal" in the strict sense, the high wall is not in Petworth terms so ancient. This stretch at least is a silent testimony to the obsession with privacy of Charles Seymour, sixth Duke of Somerset and master of Petworth some three centuries ago.

Earlier maps and surveys are clear enough about buildings on the western side; Ralph Treswell's 1610 map showing some fourteen tenements on the west side extending from the present Hampers Green lodges as far as St. Mary's Church. John Ederton's 1541 rent return to Henry VIII names at least one of these tenements: Tobias Badmering's cottage and garden known as "Skares". John Badmering held this by the time of the Estate Survey of 1575 while, by the time of Treswell's map, the tenant is again Tobias Badmering, grandson no doubt of the first Tobias. Treswell shows too a corresponding ribbon of houses on the east side; Florence Gibson's tenement with garden, mentioned in the 1575 survey as bordering on Thomas Smyth's garden, could be on either side. A marginal note on the survey states that by 1654 Florence's house had been pulled down. The great house itself was no doubt screened to an extent by trees but a significant note is sounded by the Manorial Court in September 1687 (PHA 3955): "We present that Daniel Watersfield has erected a stable on part of land overlooking the Lord of the Manor in North Street." This was not something that Charles Seymour would readily tolerate. Trees were not protection enough; stone and mortar would replace them, not immediately but in due course of time.

Modern North Street does not encourage such reveries: for the endless stream of cars and lorries the street is a means to an end rather than an entity in its own right. Historically however North Street is perhaps Petworth's most influential street and even today is Petworth's main artery. Certainly it is far less populated now than it was in Victorian times, as a look at the census records will confirm, but cramped housing was not of course peculiar to North Street: in those days it was virtually a dormitory street for the Leconfield Estate. There are more private houses now as the Leconfield Estate gradually withdraws within the wall and houses no longer required for a severely reduced workforce pass through a natural cycle of decline, renovation and resale. Private houses as opposed to estate cottages there always were, but not too many and concentrated toward the top of the hill. North House was Dr. Hope's residence as the century turned. Preyste House is probably one of several houses of that name over the centuries. A "Prestyhouse" was sold by William White to John Morris in 1531, while an early seventeenth century conveyance talks of a messuage, barn and garden called Priesthouse in the North Street of Petworth. Some think the Priesthouse was the Rector's home in those days before the Rectory was built. I do not know. Glebe Villas, halfway up, is a row of four houses built on the site of a large ruinous premises in the 1890s at the instigation of Mrs. Holland, the then rector's wife. PHA 6314

Troops in North Street 1906. *Mr. and Mrs C. Knox, Hangleton.*

gives a plan showing the post and rail fence in 1804 much as it is today, although of course the buildings have changed. PHA 6314 recounts that a cricket bat had been hurled through a window apparently by members of a party leaving the Masons' Arms one night. The Earl of Egremont is backing William Stoner, one of his tenants, in seeking counsel's advice on an action for malicious damage, or worse! His Lordship's hope is that such action "will prevent a repetition and increase of these practices which prevent the peaceable inhabitants of the town from remaining quiet in their beds". Rowdy behaviour, as any delving into court records soon shows, is not an exclusively modern prerogative. Samuel Garland, one of the suspects, is noted as a ringleader and of a "democratic and bad disposition".

In a less breathless age than this there were shops scattered the length of North Street, not just the present concentration of antique dealers in the ancient houses at the top of the hill. The premises on the corner were outfitters for nearly a century until the mid-1980s, Collins, Gallop, Kensett, then for many years F. G. Fox. Previous to that Mrs. Burnett had sold toys and fancy goods. Its turn of the century neighbours were a butcher and a clock specialist. Did Mr. Steadman make clocks or simply repair them? He certainly attended to the church clock and looks now a final lingering link with Petworth's immemorial tradition as a clockmaking centre. Down the hill there was a pub, the Wheatsheaf, where the road bends and the white post and rail fence begins. The building is age-old but the pub cannot be traced back beyond mid-Victorian times. It seems formerly to have been a tenement called Westlands. In the earlier century a favourite stopping-place for cyclists, it closed in 1959. Even in the 1950s it would have had to rely on customers on foot; parking space it had none. Even more ephemeral was the Running Horse further down, half-timbered and end-on to the road. Nothing more elevated than a beer house, it flourished in early Victorian times.

North Street before the motor car was long and quiet: one might see young ladies taking a decorous turn on their bicycles, or Walter Dawtrey's thoroughbreds from Golden Square being given their exercise, one ridden, one led, the sound of hooves re-echoing against the high wall. On Sundays the outlying farmers would come up in their carts, eschewing church for chapel. Between the wars Yankee Ayling would come up with his donkey from Limbo far out on the London Road. It would be pension day. Well might a schoolboy returning years later to Petworth wonder how every morning he had bowled his iron hoop down the main road beside the wall, with never a qualm.

As the schoolboys no doubt found, North Street is a long street; in fact the junction with the Horsham Road is not more than a hundred and eighty years old. The new road was provided by the Earl of Egremont in 1813 to link up with a much older route to the Fox Inn. An older Petworth looked below the junction and down beyond the Masons' Arms to the turnpike gate. The Masons' Arms goes back at least to 1780 and was formerly known as Vinsons after an early landlord, probably the first. The pub was formerly three cottages known collectively as "Smiths". For a brief period this century the pub was known as "The Trap" before reverting once more to its old title. Here was a convenient stopping place for charabancs on their way to Goodwood, a last port of call before Goodwood itself. Mr. Martin at the Masons would send travellers over to Mrs. Exall opposite for tea and hot water for washing – very necessary in days of open charabancs with solid tyres.

Abutting onto the Mason's Arms was the workhouse, built in the early eighteenth century and claimed by E. V. Lucas to be, with the exception of Battle, the most attractive in Sussex. Indeed with the exception mentioned, "It is the only pretty workhouse I remember". "Pretty" seems an odd appellation for a workhouse. The Petworth institution survived until the early 1930s and the building was afterward used as a private school. A garage now stands on the site, the workhouse having been pulled down in the late 1950s. One must feel that if the building had survived a few years more it would probably have survived indefinitely. Architecturally its removal was a severe loss to Petworth. In older days one might imagine its very position at the bottom of the long hill by the turnpike gate as a kind of symbolism. You could fall no further without falling out of the town altogether. To be in the workhouse was indeed to be at the bottom of life's hill. George Garland, Petworth's resident photographer for some fifty years from the early 1920s, took a series of pictures of the workhouse in operation immediately prior to its closure and these are, as far as I know, the only such pictures that survive in Sussex. Not a subject for the average photographer of the period perhaps, social realism and the documentary concept being a somewhat later development. George Garland was working to an individual commission and in this case an unusually far-sighted one.

Thomas Arnop's indenture on taking over as overseer of the workhouse in 1763 is still extant (O & A 1385). It is clear that at this time the workhouse was looked upon as a utility to be farmed for profit; the benefit of the inmates fitting a little uneasily into this framework. For five shillings paid in hand and a rate levied at two shillings and sixpence in the pound Thomas Arnop binds himself to provide for seven years at Petworth workhouse "such good wholesome and sufficient meat, drink, washing, lodging, wearing apparel and anything else thought proper by the churchwardens" for all persons "now maintained, kept, clothed or otherwise receiving any kind of support whatsoever from the said parish of Petworth". The recompense would come from the work performed by the inmates.

Later memories of the workhouse survive but are fading fast: in latter years one suspects the workhouse had a higher ratio of vagrants or tramps to permanent residents than it had had in its heyday. Male (or female) tramps would arrive during the evening; their names and next destination would be entered in the register. Usually they would simply be moving on to the next workhouse at East Preston. They would be given a hot bath, a mug of tea and some bread and butter. The dormitories consisted of rows of wooden bunks, each with a rope pulley enabling the bunk to be raised for cleaning purposes. The men worked outside with goggles and a hammer breaking stones for the roads, while the women picked oakum, i.e. unravelled tarred rope to be used in upholstery. It was a familiar journey for local contractors to bring stone from quarries like Little Bognor to Petworth workhouse. The workhouse also had a great iron cage where the town's rubbish was burned and the fire was reputed never to go out. Petworth had several private refuse collections then, all apparently bringing their cargoes to the workhouse for disposal. The high-sided waggons are still remembered. The clinkered ash was used for road-building, while local

Petworth Workhouse about 1930. *Photograph by George Garland. Garland Collection.*

farmers would collect the loose ash to mix with superphosphate when drilling mangels. It was the custom to hand over an ounce of "baccy" to secure the inmates' good-will before loading.

Just beyond the turnpike gate lay Donkey Row, old cottages of character long replaced by a terrace of four built in a more pragmatic style. These have themselves grown old but without acquiring the charisma that their predecessors now appear to have had – at least in retrospect! In truth in latter days they appear to have been somewhat ruinous. Working back up the North Street from the workhouse (Harwood's Garage) and the Masons' Arms there is the site of the old Boys' School, destroyed by enemy action at Michaelmas 1942. There was heavy loss of life and the disaster cast its shadow over Petworth for decades. To an extent it still does. The communal grave is in the Horsham Road cemetery and there is a book of remembrance in St. Mary's Church. The school had been founded by the Third Earl of Egremont in 1816 for thirty boys. Laundry Cottages on the junction recall Lord Leconfield's private laundry, a world of flat irons, beeswax, hard soap, scrubbing brushes, mangles and reddened elbows, the dirty laundry coming down from the House in big wicker baskets.

Opposite Laundry Cottages, and just before the Horsham Road runs into North Street, are the Egremont Almshouses, roughly on the site of an ancient copyhold called Sopers and often referred to simply as the "Lower Hospital" to distinguish this almshouse from Somerset Hospital up the hill and into Petworth. The Lower Hospital is another foundation of George O'Brien, Third Earl of Egremont, having been endowed in 1836 with the then princely sum of £3,150. After a period of relative neglect the almshouses are now refurbished and restored.

One of the distinctive features of Petworth is the number and munificence of its almshouses and North Street is very much their home territory. "No town in Sussex", wrote Arnold in 1864, "is better provided". Thompson's Hospital, a little further into Petworth, is an ancient foundation dating from 1624 and owing its name to one Thomas Thompson of Barnards Inn. Originating from Petworth, Thomas remembered his old home town in prosperous exile. Like the Egremont Almshouses, Thompson's had fallen into some decay but in 1978 the cement rendering was removed to reveal

Boys walking to school about 1900. Glebe Villas on left.

the original local stone walls and the interior was completely refurbished. Where before the accommodation had been for fourteen elderly persons in single rooms, it now comprises six flatlets and a warden's maisonette. The old Hospital had had ground floor rooms that were entered straight from the road. All were very uniform with old-fashioned barred fireplaces and a side oven. Each room had a tiny scullery on one side and bedroom on the other.

Documentation on the earlier history of Thompson's is conspicuously lacking although the charter survives at least as a copy. The following memorandum from 1806 gives some idea of contemporary attitudes. As a prayer card from Sutton workhouse succinctly puts it, "The duty of the poor and their interest are the same".

Petworth, July 19th. 1806.

AT THE ANNUAL GENERAL MEETING OF THE TRUSTEES AND VISITORS OF THOMPSON'S HOSPITAL.

The question of displacing, ruling, ordering and governing the Poor in the Hospital, being now considered, according to the Resolution of the last General Meeting: IT IS AGREED — That no one be a proper Object of this Charity, who is not a Religious, Moral, Orderly Person: It is therefore resolved;– That if any of the Poor in the said Hospital shall not be regular in their attendance on Church (viz. twice on Sundays, and on Wednesdays and Fridays also, unless prevented by Illness) Or if proof may be brought of their Drunkenness, Profaneness, or Immorallity, or of their Turbulence and Misconduct, so as to anywise disturb the Peace and Comfort of others in the Hospital: Every Person so offending shall be summoned before a Meeting of the Trustees and Visitors; and for the first Offence, shall be admonished; for the second Offence, shall be suspended from a Quarter's Payment; and for the third Offence, shall be displaced.

Somewhat paternalistic perhaps to present day tastes but likely enough those who had once attained the comparatively safe haven of Thompson's in an insecure age would not find these conditions excessively onerous.

Somerset, the "Upper Hospital" has also been much renovated of late years. It has the benefit of a healthy endowment and now admits the spouse of a lady pensioner, an alteration requiring a formal change in the original charter. Intended at first as a home for twelve poor widows, the complement increased to twenty-five in 1818. Arnold, writing in 1864, seems to have had access to surviving unwritten traditions about his Grace's visits to the site to inspect the renovations well over a century before. He paints a vivid picture of the Duke arriving in a richly carved, gilded and velvet-lined sedan chair carried by two very tall, muscular attendants each well over six feet tall. The Duke was accompanied also by a running footman carrying a silver-topped staff to clear the way and two other men who walked, one on each side of the window of the chair, poised to use the silver-headed sticks they carried to deter any person whose curiosity might tempt him to seek a glimpse of the chair's ducal occupant. Some have thought that Charles Seymour built the Hospital but records at Petworth House show that it had been originally a private house. In 1728 His Grace had bought a "capital messuage" in North Street and two houses to the south from the heirs of John Cook. The house had been let out and was tenanted at this time by a Mrs. Wickliffe.

Material concerning the Hospital preserved in Petworth House Archives is very extensive; not only are there detailed accounts, but also admission applications which throw much light on social conditions a hundred and fifty years ago and more. In an average year the agent at Petworth House might receive some half a dozen petitions for a pension "either out of the House or in it" as the expression went. An in-pensioner received £20 per annum in addition to accommodation, while an out-pensioner received a proportion of surplus income. Ann Knight of Petworth made a successful application in 1846, the census records mentioning her as in residence at the Hospital in 1851 and 1861. A widow at the time of her application, Ann had learned and practised midwifery at the Hospital in Brownslow Street in London for two years, beginning work as a midwife in Petworth in 1804. In the intervening years she had attended some 4,800 confinements in Petworth and adjacent parishes with just five fatal cases in all that time. She could produce her book with the name of each person, place of residence and the date. Being now in her seventieth year she is no longer equal to the fatigue and anxiety of a midwife's lot.

Rebecca Hatfull would appear rather less likely to have her request granted but her petition gives a fascinating glimpse of a larger world. A former schoolmistress, she is the widow of Edward Hatfull a former purser in the Royal Navy. He had sailed with Captain Bligh in search of the mutineers from the Bounty and afterward in the Vesuvius. During the mutiny at Spithead he had served in the Latona under Captain Legge helping in "bringing the men to their duty". He had later served with Captain Duff in the Mars and had been with Duff when he was killed at Trafalgar in 1805.

Hatfull had retired on half-pay and set up as a Navy Agent, but when his business failed in 1815 he had left his wife and gone to America. Mrs. Hatfull had kept a small school near Portsmouth for some fifteen years but a nervous complaint that had its origin in excitement and anxiety had gradually grown worse until she became a helpless cripple. When her husband died in 1829 she received a naval pension of £30 a year and settled first at Haslemere, then at Northchapel. Mrs. Hatfull now finds her pension quite insufficient. Perhaps she was allowed an outpension but one doubts whether her Petworth connections would have been strong enough to sway Colonel Wyndham's agent in her favour.

Somerset Lodge next to the Hospital is described by Nairn as "the nicest house in Petworth". Ironic that in 1956 an application was approved to demolish it! *The Southern Weekly News*, in reporting the decision to demolish, inadvertently accompanied it with a picture of Somerset Hospital and had to print a retraction the following week to allay the consternation of Hospital residents. Unlike Petworth workhouse, Somerset Lodge was finally reprieved. The house bears the date 1653 although some features suggest a slightly earlier period. Long in the possession of the Mose family, the Lodge passed to a kinsman John Jewkes, no doubt the same John Jewkes MP who inherited Stringers Hall from his cousin John Cook in 1726. It was bought by the Duke of Somerset in 1740 and conveyed to the trustees of Somerset Hospital in 1747. They let out the property for several decades until putting it up for auction at the Angel Inn in 1799 to raise money to redeem Land Tax on the

# NORTH STREET

Cyclists in North Street about 1900. Thompsons Hospital on left.
*Photograph by Walter Kevis. Garland Collection.*

Hospital Estates. In default of adequate bids for the property the Earl of Egremont bought it back for £250. Not until the present century would the house revert to private ownership.

In leaving North Street it is appropriate to look once more to the green fields that appeared so tantalisingly between the houses as we came up the long hill. As the evening sun bathes the slopes it throws into relief the distinctive man-made ridges that are the remains of Petworth's town-field system. This contiguity with its ancient field-system makes Petworth now unique among the towns of the Sussex Weald. These ridges were age-old when John Quixley, the rector, clashed with the great house over his right to drive pigs down North Street to pasture east of the Kirdford road as the other tenants did. Richard Lynne the elder and others would testify before the manorial court in 1447 that the rectors of Petworth had indeed had, of old time, the right to drive their pigs down the road to their traditional pasturage (PHA). One last thought to accompany us on our way round Petworth: the Manorial Survey of 1882 marks near the top of the hill a copyhold called Stradlings and the "White Horse Inn". These names mean little now but act as a salutary reminder of how much there is that we do not know, shall not know, and perhaps can never know.

# 2

## CHURCH STREET

CHURCH Street seems now somewhat forlorn, hardly a street at all. There is little feeling of being lived in, and on one side there is only the green churchyard grass. In the season there will be a queue on the pavement waiting for entry to Petworth House, perhaps the occasional coach parked uneasily by the pavement. It will not stay for long. In the winter the wind veers shrewdly round the junction of North Street and East Street and the visitors are no more. Church Street reverts to being just an arm of the one-way system; vital rather than significant. Cars hurtle round the corner by the entrance to Petworth House stables, and crossing the road from Lombard Street to the Church is an operation of precision and no little speed. Church Street, like Park Road which joins it, is a solitary street, keeping its own counsel and, in its own way, forbidding.

It was not always so. Church Street (or Church Stile Street) was once the very heart of Petworth. Imagine the church hemmed in with houses, either side of the church gates. There had been houses in the churchyard from earliest times and they are clearly shown on Treswell's great map of 1610. Here stood the Blue Lion (formerly Springalls), mentioned as early as 1637 in Petworth House deeds. Widow Sadler was proprietress here in 1683 while, a few years later, in 1691, another proprietress, Elizabeth Holloway, was amerced by the manorial court for not grinding her barley at the Lord's mill. As the court observed a decade later, "The Lord and Lady of this Manor do keep up a mill called Coutersoal Mill for the convenience and service of the tenants" (PHA 3955). Illicit mills incurred the court's displeasure. In later years the Blue Lion reverted to being a private house and for decades was the home of James Goldring the schoolmaster (Beck *Inns* 143).

William Bullaker deposing before a Chancery commission in 1596 regarding Petworth as he remembered it some forty years earlier when he was a boy, recalled "in his childehoode goinge to schoole in Petworth". He came from well-to-do Chichester Roman Catholic stock and Petworth seems at first sight an odd choice for his schooling. Was the school, as schools so often were, attached to the parish church? A terrier of 1635, preserved in separate copies both in the Chichester Diocesan records and at Petworth House, speaks of "the churchyard and a tenement therein standinge used for a schoole house". It was not unusual at this time to have a school closely connected with a church building, sometimes in a kind of porch or narthex, an open cloister built on to the church itself. It is possible that Ralph Treswell's 1610 map shows some such building tagged on to the church. On the other hand, we may look to a building Treswell shows tucked in under the left hand wall. The truth is that we simply do not know. We can say only that the school would have had a high reputation in the 1550s or Bullaker would never have been sent there.

A quite different school was that built for thirty girls at the beginning of the nineteenth century. Once again it was a foundation of the Earl of Egremont. The school lay to the west of the church gate but not as far along as the corner. The building on the immediate left of the church gates was a tenement anciently known as Brittains. In the course of time the girls school removed to East Street and the former Independent chapel there was converted to educational use. It continued as a girls' school until the mid twentieth century. Bryants the stationers at the end of the road also moved to new premises in East Street, a shop adjoining what would later become the "new" Post Office. Bryants' Church Street premises were demolished in 1872 to make way for the present Church Lodge at Petworth House, while the girls' school would appear to have been demolished at some time previous to this.

Two photographs of these alterations survive, one showing Bryants the stationers before demolition, the other the building reduced to rubble and the vista to Petworth House briefly opened up. These views are some of the few extant prints of Francis Gaudrion Morgan, Petworth's first photographer. Morgan had been, as the old photographers so often were, primarily a chemist. Petworth born, he trained in London but returned to his home town to practise. In later years he would retire to Brighton where he died in 1894. Curiously in his later Petworth years he does not seem to have kept up his photography, all his known work appearing to predate the arrival of Walter Kevis in 1878. Morgan's house and premises were immediately east of the church gate but he also had a studio in Bartons Lane. On Morgan's retirement, G. H. Edgar took over the chemist's business and it passed eventually to Mr. Steggles. The chemists transferred to Market Square when the remaining houses in the churchyard were demolished. Another refugee from Church Street at this time was Mr. Letchford whose boot shop moved to the corner of Saddlers Row, a position his successors still hold today. The house at the eastern end of the row had once belonged to the parish and is sometimes mentioned in the proceedings of the Vestry Committee, a nineteenth century precursor of today's Parish Council. In May 1810 an order was made to erect a building at the north end of the parish house occupied by James Edwards and adjoining the churchyard. The structure would house the town's new fire engine. In April 1822 it was ordered that the engine be looked to and the pipes oiled immediately, and this in future to be done by the overseer a week before or after each quarter day.

In December 1826 the engine required: one 20 foot pipe and five 40 foot pipes, all at 2/2d per foot with a 12 foot suction pipe at 4/6d a foot, not including the brass and six joints at 10/- a joint. A round total of some £30. The Vestry decided to buy the suction pipe as being essential to the use of the engine but in view of the fact that the Parish had in the past expended large sums on the engine and pipes, resolved to apply to the various local insurance offices to defray the cost of the other pipes. It is not known how successful this was. Probably the great fire at Burton House on the night of December 5th 1826 had exposed deficiencies in the Parish fire engine. A list is extant of some thirty three men who went to Burton on that night. James Kingshott was the fire officer, James Lucas and William Short the engine men and William Gearing the coachman. A colophon reads: "Lord Egremont's Engine went away although Mr. Bassett wished it to remain longer. The Parish Engine did remain as long as was required and checked the flames whenever they broke out again which happened in several instances". Mr. Bassett was majordomo at Burton House at the time. Obviously with a manual apparatus a large force was needed so that those who became exhausted by their labours could be relieved.

The houses in the churchyard were demolished at the turn of the present century. At this distance in time it is difficult to ascertain the reason, but certainly with them went much of the character of Church Street. The land on which they stood remains unconsecrated and it was on part of this ground that the War Memorial was erected by public subscription in 1921. In these days of urban infilling, much of it highly undesirable, it is ironic that this historic settlement is, and will no doubt remain, open.

Opposite the church gates and on the right hand as one comes up Lombard Street is the old house known formerly as Pettifers. The distinctive large stone building forms, as Arnold says, "two sides of a square: one side facing the church, the other Lombard Street". The building has retained much of its character, escaping the Georgian modification that other less imposing residences have acquired. One feature however is now lacking, as Constance Lady Leconfield lamented, "The old house opposite the Church in Church Street, now Tudor House, occupied in 1867 by Mr. Green the grocer, had its old Elizabethan windows then, but they were replaced by modern ones in the eighties and the house irretrievably spoiled" (*Random Papers* 1938 p.p. 45–6).

Pettifers is traditionally considered the ancient town house of the Dawtrey family from Moor a couple of miles from Petworth, but in fact there is no trace of the Dawtreys in the long recorded history of this site. It seems more likely that the Manorial Survey Map of 1882 is correct in locating the Dawtrey residence slightly to the east where East Street and Church Street meet. According to some notes prepared by Miss G. M. A. Beck, formerly archivist at Petworth House, in 1954, the first mention of the site at Petworth House comes in 1573. In 1590 Robert Colbrooke, mercer, of Chichester, made over to John Smith a messuage now or lately occupied by John Bywimble "right over against the church gate which leadeth from the Church to the Market Place". In 1622 the house was sold to the Stringer family, passing eventually to Richard Cooke, a cousin. The Stringer and Cooke families owned both Pettifers and Stringers Hall in East Street all through this period. The descent continued largely by cousins through the Jewkes and Mose families until the house was sold to Lord Egremont in 1782. We have already met some of

Petworth Town Band in Church Street about 1900. Houses and shops still hide the churchyard.

these important eighteenth-century Petworth families in connection with Somerset Lodge in North Street.

At the time of its sale in 1782 Pettifers was divided into two, one part being occupied by Robert Palmer, mercer and the other by William Trew, tallow-chandler. In 1786 Thomas Green, tallow-chandler, presumably successor to John Trew, bought the house, then described as part dwelling-house used by Green, part warehouse used by Robert Palmer. Palmer died in 1787 aged eighty-seven but the Palmer family are later to be found at Avenings in Golden Square. Thomas Green died in 1813 to be succeeded by his son Thomas and he in turn by Thomas' son James, the firm eventually becoming W. and H. Green. It so continued until taken over by Otways early this century.

Greens were an old-fashioned grocers who were still in touch with their origins as tallow-chandlers, much of their stock being what we would now class as hardware. A number of the firm's customer order books survive, the page illustrated coming from October 1882. Oxtail is oxtail soup, com.tumblers are of course common tumblers. Oswego is a biscuit, petroleum would no doubt be used for lighting. Accounts were more leisurely then, this one coming to £68.12.11½d for the six months to the end of the year. Mr. Dearling, whose book this is, brought in eggs and butter and what he brought in was recorded in the back of the account book and set against his grocery bill. Mr. Dearling's accounting seems to have been quite as leisurely as Messrs. Green's!

Pettifers had the older name of Bywimbles, it being originally home to the Bywimble family, prominent in late sixteenth and early seventeenth century Petworth. John Bywimble senior, although blind, had acted as bailiff and rent collector for the Manor in the 1560s, while his son John seems to have set up on his own as a mercer. A vivid sidelight on the use of Bywimbles as a shop at this time is provided by a church court case from 1603; depositions from three witnesses being preserved among diocesan papers at the West Sussex Record Office. Margaret Goodman, wife of a prominent innkeeper in the town, is suing Thomas Westdeane for defamation i.e. accusing Westdeane of putting her public reputation in jeopardy by making slanderous statements about her which he is unable to substantiate. Joanna Curtis had actually been in John

A page from Thomas Dearling's 1882 W. H. Green order book.

Bywimble's shop buying of wares when she heard Margaret Goodman and Thomas Westdeane coming "through the streete of Petworth" close by the shop. There was, it seemed, some discord or at least "some angrie words betwixt them". Margaret was not honest, cried Westdeane, she was a whore. When Margaret called in Joanne Curtis and others as witnesses Westdeane said, "Thou art an arrante whore and came from Greenwich", apparently a reference to Greenwich as a haunt of seafaring men. William Mose had been in the shop, and Mark Upfield too had been at work there at his trade as a tailor; both re-echo Joanna Curtis' evidence. Thomas Westdeane does not appear to defend the case and it is likely that the consistory court would have upheld Margaret Goodman's complaint. Thomas Westdeane would be fined and quite possibly sentenced to perform public penance wearing a white sheet for his "incontinence" i.e. his failure to control his tongue.

On the opposite corner of Lombard Street from Pettifers alias Bywimbles, lay the ancient site of the Crown Inn, carefully described in the Petworth Register as "near ye church gate, ye corner house on the left hand coming up from ye Market". This with other properties was a part of Richard Ayre's Charity, a benefaction made in 1673, and yielding some £16 annually to be used for gifts to the poor, or simply to be distributed in the form of bread (Arnold p. 84). The building, used as a bakery at the close of the nineteenth century, was destroyed by fire in 1899. Remnants' Fire, as it was known after the last tenants, made a great impression on the town and was remembered with awe for decades, Petworth Fire Brigade being effectively helpless once the blaze had gained a hold. It may well be this fire to which Lord Egremont refers (*Wyndham and Children First* p. 67), when Uncle Reggie combined his own aristocratic efforts with those of the Petworth House private fire-engine in an effort to redeem the situation. "Have a care, Mr. Reggie," urged Mr. Sutton, Clerk of the Works, as the jet from the Petworth House engine bade fair to create havoc rather than contain it. Mr. Remnant had been in the habit of assisting members of St. Mary's congregation by cooking their joints and vegetables for dinner using the ovens in which, on weekdays, he baked the bread. His patrons would collect their Sunday roast when they emerged from divine service. After the demise of Remnants' bakery this invaluable role was taken over by Mr. Knight just down the road in Lombard Street.

A markworthy feature of the premises before the great fire had been the large first floor room looking out onto Lombard Street. It had apparently been the chief apartment of the long forgotten Crown Inn and boasted a most unusual ceiling. Arnold writes of its "elaborate ornaments in plaster boldly but somewhat roughly executed. Men, women and various animals are represented in grotesque attitudes, some of the figures are but little injured. On the space above the fireplace, between it and the ceiling is a coat of arms with a shield, having on it a boar's head, which also appears elsewhere on the plaster. The crest and supporters are mutilated" (Arnold p. 84).

The premises were rebuilt and taken by Ernest Streeter who had begun in business in 1888 opposite the Swan Hotel, but moved a year later to a shop in Golden Square. In the course of time his daughter Peggy insisted on being made a partner rather than simply being treated as an assistant, hence the unusual name E. Streeter and Daughter. Ernest Streeter was well-known as a dealer in quality antiques, but was also a link with Petworth's ancient horological traditions, taking a special interest in timepieces of all kinds and going round to large houses in the locality to wind and regulate the clocks and undertake repairs and restorations. The following note from *Views and Reviews*, p.p. 18–19 gives a good idea of the scope of his business. It reflects his sojourn in Golden Square but is more appropriate here because it was the Church Street premises that would come to be inseparably connected with him.

MR. E. STREETER, PRACTICAL WATCH AND CLOCK MAKER, JEWELLER, SILVERSMITH AND DEALER IN ANTIQUES, MARKET SQUARE, PETWORTH

The business carried on by Mr. Streeter at the above address was established by its present proprietor five years ago, and its progress, commercially speaking, has been of a most gratifying character. The premises are eligibly situated, being in the very heart of the town, and in near proximity to all the principal places of business interest — the Town Hall, the general post office, the London and County

Bank, the Half Moon Hotel and other prominent establishments. The building is a picturesque edifice of three storeys, possessing a double frontage on the ground floor of some forty feet in extent, the plate glass windows affording a superior means of displaying a fine assortment of valuable articles, including watches, clocks, jewellery, silver and electro plated wares, bric-a-brac, bronzes, ivories, enamels and antiques in great variety. Few will pass this interesting emporium without at least stopping to admire the singularly rich assortment of goods which Mr. Streeter's windows display. As a watch and clock maker, the proprietor of this establishment is unsurpassed in the town, the good quality of his horological instruments being recognised by all who have had the good fortune to become possessed of them. Mr. Streeter constantly keeps in stock a large assortment of every kind of watch and clock, from the costly chronometer and delicately constructed repeater, down to the modest silver watch which can be purchased for a comparative trifle; and from the cheap cottage alarm clock, priced at a few shillings, to the elegant bronze, marble, gilt, or ormolu timepiece, upon which a wealth of artistic effort has been expended. The jewellery department is well cared for, and the display of goods, shielded by the glass cases on the counter, and at rear, is rich, varied and fully up-to-date in excellence of design, beauty of workmanship and quality of material. A choice collection of silver and plated ware is kept, including spoons and forks, entrée dishes, table plate of every description, and other articles too numerous to recapitulate. There is also a fair subsidiary stock of goods in the optical department, including spectacles, eye-glasses, pince-nez, opera glasses, field glasses, marine glasses and all things pertaining to this department. Passing to a handsome show-room on the first floor one finds a choice assortment of antique furnishings, bric-a-brac, *objets d'art*, pictures by many of the most renowned old masters, and a hundred other interesting items, in which the collector and connoisseur would certainly take delight. Mr. Streeter has proved a successful restorer of faded and injured oil paintings, and in this line enjoys a wide-spread patronage. He is also a competent judge of Art metal work, cabinet goods of the Jacobean, Queen Anne, Chippendale, Seriton, Adams, Hepplewhite, and other periods, and as a dealer in the charming old grandfather clocks, now so greatly in vogue among aristocratic collectors, he has a high and far reaching reputation. Repairs in all departments are undertaken and carried out by competent workmen, who act under the personal supervision of the

CHURCH STREET

Remembrance Sunday about 1955. *Photograph by George Garland. Garland Collection.*

proprietors. With such favourable facilities for meeting the varied requirements of customers, it need not surprise the reader to learn that the house in question has achieved so sound a position in the commercial system of the district. Mr. Streeter undertakes contracts for the winding of clocks, and the keeping of the same in thorough repair.

The Streeter tradition in clocks, watches and jewellery is still carried on in part of the premises by Anne Simmons, a former employee of Miss Streeter.

Looking back over a lifetime spent working in the Church Street premises, Peggy Streeter could recall workmen taking down the big iron railings that marked off the churchyard. They were borne away to be used for munitions during the Great War. When the railings were still in position sheep grazed in the churchyard to keep the grass short. She vividly remembered too the visit of Queen Mary to the Church Street shop between the wars, Lady Leconfield having earlier sent over a message to say that she would be bringing Her Majesty, a great enthusiast for antiques. Messrs. Streeter were pleased to sell Her Majesty an ancient tea-caddy and a gold and ivory patch-box. There were antique shops in Petworth then – if not quite as many as now!

The obelisk in the middle of the road where the three streets converge was designed by Barry and his original drawings for it survive although not, as one might have expected, in Petworth House Archives. Originally of course the obelisk carried gas lamps. It was put up by the citizens of the town as a mark of gratitude to the great house for the provision of gas for the inhabitants. Sadly now it is in some disrepair and badly needs restoring, the oxidation of the ironwork having dislodged the stonework. With the church gates, also reputedly designed by Barry, themselves in some disrepair, obelisk and gates form a feature of Petworth which is at once characterful and badly neglected.

# 3

## PARK ROAD

I HAVE taken Park Road to begin at the right angle bend where Bacons the shoe shop now have their premises, although some would see this particular stretch of road as a continuation of Pound Street. An old name is Back Road but it is not in essence one of the oldest Petworth thoroughfares, owing its existence largely to the building of Lord Leconfield's stables and the demise of West Street. The high wall is always on the left, broken only by the opening that leads into the Leconfield Estate Office and the huge wooden doors of the Grand Entrance to Petworth House. Nairn writes of "two eighteenth century piers surmounted by macabre trophies beautifully carved — armour and helmets without any men inside them . . . very eerie and very un-English". The concept of Gog and Magog is Hebraic in origin, the twin figures symbolizing unknown and unnumbered barbaric hordes and their threat to the established order and all its values. Then comes the high stable wall and, eventually, and opposite, the suffering backs of Lombard Street houses, suffering of course from the grime of heavy traffic in a confined space.

It seems hardly right to call Park Road "a street"; it is more a sacrifice to the internal combustion engine. Like its continuation Church Street it is a vital link in the one-way system, almost as if its sole purpose were to speed the north and east bound traffic out of the town as quickly as possible: out of sight, out of mind. If Petworth were a railway system then Park Road would be the tunnel. All too often however, a line of cars building up in Pound Street announces another blockage. Something large is having difficulty on the tight corner by the stables. Soon engines are throbbing all the way up Pound Street and as far down Station Road as the eye can see; aggrieved motorists clamber from their cars as if transported suddenly and disconcertingly to an alien dimension. Those with local knowledge reverse into unlikely recesses and set off southward to circumnavigate Petworth another way. Those who do not have that knowledge are wiser to stay put. White lines in the road as the stable wall curves warn drivers of larger vehicles to give themselves room for manoeuvre: great gashes in the stables brickwork like bleeding open flesh show that they do not always do so.

Despite, or perhaps because of, the traffic, Park Road is the most solitary of all Petworth's streets, not silently lamenting the loss of her old importance like Church Street, but simply left alone. Few people walk this way; strangers who have missed a more orthodox way to Petworth House perhaps: you would not really expect to find Petworth residents walking in Park Road. There is no pavement and other, more accessible, streets fulfil a similar function. Even the great stables turn their back on Park Road and the Leconfield Estate keeps its own counsel. Just one thing can transfigure Park Road and that is the sun shafting down between the high walls.

The great stables, worthy descendants of palatial ancestors in the Park itself, are empty now and the cobbled yard has recently seen service as a visitors' car park for Petworth House. Out of season they are quite silent, a kind of memorial to an age of horses. From those massive gates would come Lord Leconfield's horses for exercise. There was no one-way system and what traffic there was could go either way at the East Street obelisk. The sound of hooves would echo and re-echo in the primal silence. There were no motor-engines then. Children would rush to windows to catch a glimpse of the horses. Ern. Carver recalled coming up from Stag Park to the Stable Yard to deliver hay. There were some three score horses in the stables and Lord Leconfield hunted six days a week: himself three and his huntsmen three. The stables also kept his Lordship's carriage horses. Mr. Barnes was in charge and no one was allowed to deliver after ten o'clock when the yard had been swept. The stables always insisted on white oats: black weren't allowed: they coloured the dung and this wasn't considered acceptable.

Tucked in on the tortuous bend stands the squat unpretentious Strict Baptist chapel, the Ebenezer. Ebenezer is Hebrew for "stone of help" and is a common enough title for Strict Baptist chapels. The name refers to a famous old Testament deliverance against the Philistines (1 Samuel vii 12). The chapel itself was erected for Isaac

Petworth House, the main entrance 1898. *Mrs Barbara Calder, Aberdeen.*

Eatherton in 1887 on ground once forming part of the ancient copyhold of Teelings in the Market Square. Eatherton kept a shoe shop in one of the old houses that stood in the churchyard but himself lived in a house that fronted on to Park Road, surviving still if no longer as a separate entity. It appears that Isaac Eatherton and his church were the lineal descendants of a much larger congregation that had met in the early century under the auspices of Benjamin Challen, the grocer, on the second floor of his premises in Golden Square. Eatherton and his little band could look back on former glories: the Golden Square chapel had seated some two hundred hearers and had been opened by William Huntington the famous evangelist. In its heyday it attracted famous independent preachers like James Hallett. A selection of Hallett's sermons, many preached at the Providence Chapel, Petworth, survives in book form.

When, through the death of Benjamin Challen's son Charles, the Independent cause in Petworth eventually lost its home, its followers fell on troublous times, meeting either in each others' homes or in some temporary accommodation. The years in the wilderness will certainly have exacted their toll and it was probably but a small group that met at the newly-built Ebenezer in 1887. Never numerically strong, and probably predominantly elderly as those who remembered the great days in Market Square would by now certainly be, the little cause was too fragile to survive and by the end of the century Isaac Eatherton's bold initiative had foundered. Services were carried on by Strict Baptist ministers until in 1911 Mr. Picknell from Redhill formed a Strict Baptist church on Isaac Eatherton's foundations.

The chapel is plain and utilitarian. Decoration is eschewed and vestments are not used, the minister wearing a dark Sunday suit. Ministers are, and have always been, supply. Petworth has never been a sufficiently flourishing cause to think of a resident minister. The heavy lorries that shake the building and briefly halt the train of thought create a special bond between minister and congregation. The pulpit rises high at the back of the large single room and below it is a raised desk used once by the deacon. Then comes a series of long pews or benches. For reasons of space there is no centre aisle. Supplementary hinged pews line the east wall. When the sun shines in through the big west windows it lights up the whole room. Links with a lost past are the scars where the old gas lamps were once fitted, and the narrow hinged additions to the pew shelves that enabled refreshments to be placed at mid-day, between morning and afternoon service. Services were held morning and afternoon so that the predominantly agricultural congregation could return home to attend to their animals in the late afternoon. This service pattern still survives in a changed world. Prayers are extempore, spoken with an immediacy now rarely found outside these rather sparse congregations. Numbers may be augmented by visiting worshippers in the summer months but the future of the little chapel looks precarious. We may echo the prayer of the minister Mr. Wood from Croydon at the centenary service in May 1987:

"We thank thee Lord for thy great goodness in maintaining thy truth in this house of prayer these one hundred years. Thy people here are diminished in number but we thank thee that the doors remain open . . . that the Gospel is preached, that thy servants continue to minister . . . We look up unto thee for a gracious reviving, that thou wilt build up the walls of Jerusalem . . . that thou wilt return in thy power among the churches".

TREAD LIGHTLY HERE

Lombard Street about 1898. Bill Knight with smock, Joe Stedman with barrow. *Photograph by Walter Kevis. Garland Collection.*

# 4

## LOMBARD STREET

LOMBARD Street, often simply called the "cobble" street, has always held a unique position: by tradition it is the quintessential Petworth street, even featuring in a nationally marketed jigsaw produced just before the outbreak of war in 1939. Lombard Street is No. 113 in the Mammoth Series, No. 112 being Westminster Abbey! "Old Petworth Village" says a rather condescending caption. The picture itself, probably redrawn from a photograph, is a little quaintified but clearly and unmistakably Lombard Street. With the removal of the church spire in 1947 it is less likely that Lombard Street would receive a similar accolade today.

The street has doubtless existed in some form, as a kind of Jacob's ladder leading from the secular brashness of the Market Square to the spiritual haven of St. Mary's, pretty well as long as Petworth has been a recognisable civic entity at all. The name Lombard Street however does not in itself appear particularly ancient. The origins of the name are obscure. Does it perhaps refer to forgotten tradesmen from Lombardy setting up residence in the street, much as glassworkers from Lorraine had settled locally in the sixteenth century? Lombard Street would then be the street of the Lombards. The difficulty with this is that no trace survives of such hypothetical settlers from Lombardy but it must be said that, given the scant information available on Lombard Street in the seventeenth and eighteenth centuries, it is not possible to be sure. The old journalistic conceit of contrasting the tranquillity of Petworth's Lombard Street with the urban bustle of its London counterpart may not go back beyond Garland press captions of the late 1920s but it is most likely that an earlier, more straightforward, comparison between the two Lombard Streets as financial and business centres to their respective communities underlies the name.

A much earlier name is "the Causey" i.e. the Causeway, still preserved in Causey Place at the very bottom of the street and the street is explicitly referred to in John Ederton's return as the Causeway, being in those days literally a narrow causeway raised above the open drain that carried the town's sewage. John Lee has a messuage and appurtenances on the causeway called Bullockerds. This property is shown on the 1882 map as comprising a sizeable portion of the lower part of the present street and extending eastward in the direction of East Street. Thomas Fourde's Bamburghs would appear to be commemorated by present-day Bamboroughs further up on the west side of the street, while William Portburie's garden called Lanye (once John Skynner's) is located by the 1882 survey about halfway up the street on the east side. Others have placed this important property adjacent to the present Daintrey House in East Street, but the old names on the 1882 map, wherever they can be checked, have always been found reliable.

Nearly into the Market Square on the west side are the premises marked on the 1882 map as Marshalls, now a newsagents. In later years there is a tradition that the Taylor family of clockmakers were here and it is quite possible that Lombard Street may have played a prominent role in the ill-documented story of Petworth clockmaking. Far earlier than this a Chancery Court deposition from 1592, preserved in Petworth House Archives, gives a vivid picture of a heated exchange of views in Elizabethan Petworth, apparently at that very spot where Lombard Street joins the Market Square. Thomas Turges, copyhold tenant of Teelings in the Market Square, had refused to pay the fine imposed by the lord of the manor for admission to his copyhold, considering it far too high: seven shillings having been increased twentyfold to seven pounds. "That is much," said an old copyholder to his Lordship's steward. "Whie," replied the steward, "do you not see what a faire house he hath younder?" (Turges' house stood on the north side of the Market Square, opposite the present Leconfield Hall.) The steward backed up his argument by pointing to Teelings to show what a fine house it was. The old man, whose name was Robert Marshall, did not take the point, retorting, "It ys very hard Mr. Steward thatt a man having noe more groundes than is belonginge to younder house or bestowing most of his wealthe upon building of an house should therefore because he hath a faire house have his fyne raised so highe." (PHA 7362 CCP p.p. 58–9.) It seems reasonable to connect this Robert Marshall with the adjacent property of Marshalls. Treswell's 1610 map does not help greatly, showing Lombard Street as simply a line of large houses, probably subdivided into tenements. A notable feature then, as to some extent now, is the extensive ground lying on the east side between Lombard Street and East Street.

Perhaps Lombard Street's most distinctive era was the early part of this century and the late years of Queen Victoria. A cluster of small shops on the east side, some too on the west side, effectively made it a village in its own right, a village set in the very centre of a small town. Mog Thayre, looking back on a long sojourn in Lombard Street, recalls what in retrospect seems now a Golden Age:

"Lombard Street was almost a little community of its own in that last decade before the Great War. There was Knights the bakers and next door Mrs. Knight the greengrocer – no relation. Further down on the same side was Dolly Westwood's (now the Blackbirds bookshop) she sold wool and haberdashery. Weavers the newsagents were then at the bottom where King and Chasemore are now. They were soon to move over to their present position. Their predecessors had been Burdens the newsagents. Bishops the shoe people were next door. Then as now there were fewer shops on the opposite side. Mr. and Mrs. Kevis who sold cigarettes and tobacco and carried on business as a photographer were tucked in on the left as you went up the cobbled street. Did I know them? Oh yes, of course I did but they did tend to keep themselves to themselves. They had no children and they left a few years after I came to Petworth. Further up in "Ebenezer Villas" was a small private school similar to that run by the Misses Austin at Boxgrove in Pound Street."

(*Petworth Society Magazine* No. 39). She well remembered Knights the bakers half-way up the east side:

"Grandad Knight, my mother's father and Uncle Arch's father too of course, was baker, confectioner, billposter and town crier, quite a curious combination. He was certainly a leading figure in Petworth life. The bakery premises have now been converted into two separate houses but in those days the bakehouse itself was at the top of the passage leading from Lombard Street. It had two doughbins and two ovens. Here too the bags of flour were stacked. Another room was known as the doughnut house, a big room with a fireplace. Here the doughnuts were made. The shop was on the right facing the street, while the sitting-room was on the left in the front.

"Grandad Knight made the muffins and crumpets himself, cooking them in the kitchen on a special stove with a flat top, perhaps some 2½ foot square. Crumpets were made in steel rings with a quite different mixture from that for muffins, the crumpet mixture being poured into the special steel rings, each greased beforehand like a cake-tin. Grandad Knight had a special jug for this. The muffin mixture however had to rise, then, when cooked, the muffins had to be lifted one by one out of the pan and the flour shaken from them, Grandad Knight had a special knife like a pallet knife for prising them out. Muffins were much larger than crumpets and a muffin should be cooked on both sides then pulled open to put the butter in the middle. Crumpets and muffins both needed retoasting and both could be cooked on a toasting fork in front of the fire. They were sold in the shop; we didn't go out with them. Another Knight speciality were their famous lardy rolls at 7 for 3d.

Grandad Knight combined the making of muffins and crumpets with being town crier, an ancient office associated in the past with keeping the market in order. It was still taken quite seriously and he had the town crier's bell. He didn't dress up but he did usually take with him notes of what he had to say. "Oh Yes, Oh Yes, Oh Yes," he'd begin and ring the bell three times. "This is to give notice . . ." and then he'd give his message. At this time it wasn't big events like the outbreak of war but rather local news about forthcoming events in the Iron Room or the Town Hall, a cricket match or something like that. The organisers would bring him the details and pay him a shilling for publicising them. The hand-bell was made of brass and had a wooden handle. Perhaps someone might have lost a brooch or an animal had strayed. Grandad Knight would give notice of it. He had a fairly set round: Petworth being rather more compact as a town then than now. He'd walk through the Square, up New Street, then up East Street to the Church. One of his ancient privileges was to collect toll from the fair-people on November 20th. The caravans in those days would park half-way up Lombard Street and I can remember seeing him go up into the caravans to collect the toll; they didn't have to pay a lot and he was usually some little time in each caravan. I expect they gave him a drink as well as the toll."

Tucked in on the left hand were 313 and 314 Lombard Street, a rare Leconfield Estate enclave, rented out between the wars at 2/9d. a week, the money being kept in a tin box and religiously put by for Audit Day. An unexpected bonus for the cottages, when electricity came to Lombard Street, was that 314 was the first Leconfield cottage to be put on supply. The Lombard Street businesses all had electricity put on so that the connections were ready to hand.

The preoccupation with the steeple view gave more prominence to the lower stretches of the street: the classic photographs showing the church spire towering over the cobbled way tend to leave the top part either in a discreet distance or hidden by the slight bend in the road. Further up on the left is another former shop that has now been turned back into a house, the bull's head tile marking the site of Payne's the Butchers. There was a slaughter house at the back in those early century days when every butcher had his own slaughter house.

Across the road is the wine merchants, despite numerous changes of ownership, possibly the longest serving commercial premises in Petworth if one leaves the inns and public houses out of account. In the early nineteenth century John Boxall was the incumbent and it is likely that the business was founded by him. *Tales of Old Petworth* recall "Boxall the spirit merchant" and others as James Eade the coachman's partisans in the battle for business waged with Pluck Robinson (*Tales* p. 41). John Boxall's day book for 1819-1829 is still extant but, while it contains some seven hundred orders for wine over that period, it does not mention spirits at all. Pigot's directory of 1826 lists Boxall as a "Wine and Spirit Merchant" so we can only assume that a separate book was kept for these. Boxall's enterprise seems to have been less a retail shop in our sense than a centre for bottling and delivery: the present shop windows were not in place in 1900, let alone in the 1820s. What perhaps surprises is the size of the orders by modern standards; effectively the book reflects a dispatch-house for wines. Cider is mentioned occasionally, for instance 55 gallons to Edward Peters the blacksmith in December 1819, but such mentions are rare: cider was not the choice of John Boxall's regular customers. One wonders if Master Sockett the Rector's cider came from Boxall's. If it did it is not recorded in the Day Book:

> "Some people give perry and call it champagne,
> Not so gives of Petworth the rector;
> 'Tis cider he tells us his vessels contain,
> but on tasting it proves to be nectar."

The rhyme is quoted by Arthur Beckett (*The Wonderful Weald* 1911 p. 354). I have always assumed that Thomas Sockett is the Rector referred to but Beckett does not in fact say so and does not give the source of the rhyme. It is more probably Charles Dunster, Sockett's scholarly predecessor, who is the rector in question.

John Boxall's regular customers were something of an elite, Mr. Stoveld the banker, Thomas Sockett the Rector, Mr. Greatham his curate, Colonel Wyndham from Sladelands, the Rev. Richard Smith at Sutton, Mr. Blagden the surgeon, John Bowyer the attorney, John Ellis the solicitor, Thomas Hale the surgeon. Almost all Boxall's local clients are to be found in the "Nobility, Gentry and Clergy" section of Pigot's 1826 directory. Some twenty of the twenty-four entries in this section are his customers and he has virtually none outside this list. His clientele outside Petworth, widespread as they are, including customers at Northchapel, West Burton, Shopwyke, Stopham, Bramshott, Blackdown, Chiddingfold, Madehurst and Tilford would all seem to come from this same social stratum.

Boxall's range is very limited by modern standards but on the other hand quantities delivered appear huge to modern eyes. "Cape Madeira" certainly from Cape Verde Islands is the staple red wine, while "Vidonia", a dry wine from the Canary Islands is the white. Port is a mainstay, sherry also, if a little less universal than port. As the decade advances West Indian Madeira makes its appearance. The Earl of Egremont would have a pipe of port periodically, less often a butt of sherry – large quantities indeed and at £120 a consignment, a very large sum in those days. Boxall was a wholesaler too, supplying John Greenfield of the Angel with a pipe of port from time to time. William Slater of the Star buys wholesale

A survivor from an older Lombard Street. Charlie Bishop in 1962.
*Photograph by George Garland. Garland Collection.*

too. Port retails at five shillings a bottle, sherry and "Vidonia" at five shillings and threepence. Madeira is two shillings a bottle less. Bottles and hampers are charged and returnable. T. Dicker is paid for making hampers to hold one, two or three dozen bottles respectively. A three dozen bottle hamper would have carried a pretty fair weight. "William" appears to be John Boxall's delivery man while, for the smaller local orders, servants or employees simply collected from the Lombard Street premises. John Boxall also made considerable use of the local carriers: Boxall or Collins the two London carriers, Botting from Pound Street or William Newell. All but Newell are listed as carriers in Pigot's directory. Deliveries for Tilford and Farnham would be left at the White Hart at Witley.

Boxall's old premises are still of course a wine-merchants; the following extract from *Views and Reviews* brings the shop up to the 1890s:

MR. H. J. GUMMER (SUCCESSOR TO FRANK STANLEY), WINE MERCHANT, LOMBARD STREET, PETWORTH.

This business has been established many years, and was, until recently, successfully conducted by Mr. Frank Stanley, who, owing to ill health, retired in January last, being succeeded by the present proprietor, Mr. H. J. Gummer. This gentleman has had twenty years' experience of the wine trade both at home and abroad, and since coming into possession of the business he has fully maintained the high reputation which it has enjoyed for so long. The premises in Lombard Street are extensive and well situated for business. The interior is well arranged and equipped with all the latest plant and appliances used in the trade. Everywhere the visitor is struck with the neatness and order with which the business is carried on. An extensive trade is controlled by the proprietor, and everything he offers is of a thoroughly sound and genuine character. From his long experience, he is perfectly familiar with the best sources of supply, and his selections are made with great judgment and an intimate acquaintance with the requirements of a high class and critical public. He keeps a large and varied stock of ports, sherries, clarets, and other foreign wines, as well as a splendid selection of cognacs, Scotch and Irish whiskies, and foreign liqueurs. Ample stocks are held of ales and stouts in cask and bottle, including all the best known names, and Mr. Gummer is the agent for Gale's, Horndean, Lambert and Norris', Arundel, and the Anglo-Bavarian Brewery Company's ales. With so many important specialities in hand, it is difficult to select a few of the special features of the house, but mention may be made of the famous Old Glenlivet blend of Highland whisky. Through his connection with some of the best houses in the trade, Mr. Gummer is enabled to supply his patrons in great variety and on very favourable terms, in fact, his prices for all goods are as low as possible consistent with sound quality.

Although the wine merchants remains, many commercial premises in Lombard Street have reverted to residential use and Lombard Street is not the commercial centre it once was. Just up the street on the left is Virginia Cottage, once Kevis's, then Earles', then finally Mr. Boss' antique shop. Here Walter Kevis practised as Petworth's photographer from 1878 to 1908 when he moved away to Surrey: his studio is still clearly visible as a wood and glass structure at the top of the house. When Kevis retired in 1908, he left his negatives, all glass of course, in the studio while his nephew, Herbert Earle took over the shop and carried on the tobacco retail business that Mrs. Kevis had looked after. The photographic part of the business Herbert Earle did not himself pursue and for a while Miss Coze came from Midhurst to take portraits by appointment. Her visits grew gradually less frequent and eventually ceased altogether. The glass negatives left behind by Walter Kevis remained undisturbed through two world wars. When Herbert Earle died the negatives were to be destroyed but when George Garland, alerted to the situation, asked to be allowed a few he was told he could have them all or none at all. Fortunately he elected to take them all, a full cartload of glass being accommodated for years in his Station Road studio and latterly at Windmill House in High Street whither he moved in the late 1950s. There were several hundred whole plate glass negatives of Petworth and the surrounding villages, the backbone of any photographic record of Petworth over the last century. There were virtually no country or agricultural pictures, almost all buildings or street scenes. Walter Kevis knew exactly what he wanted to do and never strayed from that. Photography was an important and integral part of his business but one that he kept firmly in its place. George

Garland saw rather less significance in the thousands of portraits, quarter-plate, half-plate, and (rarely), whole-plate that were an unlooked-for part of Herbert Earle's involuntary legacy to him. Each one has the name written in pencil across the brown envelope that holds it, sometimes the date, sometimes not. Kevis' sprawling forward hand is unmistakable. Once in George Garland's care the portraits survived precariously in cardboard orange boxes, first at the Studio, then for years in an outhouse at Windmill House. Eventually with the other Petworth negatives they were transferred to Petworth House for safe keeping. Under the terms of George Garland's will they remain there in the custody of the West Sussex Records Office. The portraits, still effectively uncatalogued, are a treasure trove of late Victorian and Edwardian costume and uniform that has yet to be fully appreciated. *News and Reviews* offers the following portrait of Walter Kevis' business in the mid-1890s. Given the somewhat adulatory tone of these advertisements "a fair measure of support" for the photographic business seems a curiously anaemic turn of phrase and may indicate that Walter Kevis looked to his trade in tobacco and sundries for a relatively high proportion of his income.

MR. W. J. KEVIS, TOBACCONIST, CIGAR DEALER, PHOTOGRAPHER AND MAKER OF PICTURE FRAMES, LOMBARD STREET, PETWORTH.

A thoroughly well established and successful trade has been developed within the past nineteen years by Mr. W. J. Kevis, whose premises are conveniently situated and commodiously adapted for carrying out on an effective scale the operations involved in the tobacco, cigar, cigarette, and tobacconist's sundries business, with which is allied the artistic business of photography and picture frame making in all their branches. The shop of Mr. Kevis, in Lombard Street, is well fitted up and replete with a comprehensive and varied assortment of high class goods, embracing all the leading lines of the cigar, cigarette and tobacco trade, the goods having been carefully selected to meet the requirements of all classes of buyers. There will be found in the stock many celebrated brands of British and foreign cigars, of Indian, Mexican, Habana, Swiss, German and Manilla makes; fancy packeted tobaccos of all the most eminent manufacturers, and cigarettes of every variety and quality. In the fancy goods department Mr. Kevis shows a capital assortment of cherry wood, briar root, meerschaum and clay pipes of all the most popular patterns, together with pouches and other sundries indispensable to the smoker's equipment, these goods being supplemented by a choice assortment of walking sticks and canes in all the newest styles and mounts. The more noteworthy specialities of this varied display include Mr. Kevis' own special "mixture," an excellent blend of the most aromatic tobacco in the market, and of super-medium strength of flavour. Mr. Kevis also conducts a photographic business, which meets with a fair measure of support both among residents in and visitors to the district. He brings to bear wide experience and a well developed artistic faculty, and on all hands favourable reports are heard of the quality of the work done. The instruments employed are of modern and up-to-date character, and all the appointments of the studio are neat and attractive, without being in any way showy or pretentious. Picture framing is carried on, and in this department very successful work is done. A wide-spread connection has been established by Mr. Kevis among the leading local residents and others. The business is well organised in each department under the personal supervision of the proprietor and his wife, and the success which attends it is a just recognition of well directed effort to cater in various capacities for the local public's convenience.

Lombard Street has changed. It will never again be as Mog Thayre remembered it, the very engine-room of Petworth's commercial life. Of all Petworth's streets it is now perhaps the quietest and ironically it is the advent of the motor-car that has made it so. Too narrow for cars to negotiate with ease, and effectively by-passed by Park Road and East Street, it lives uneasily in the age of the superstore. Some shops have reverted to residential use, others remain. Lombard Street was more sure of itself and its identity when hooves echoed and re-echoed on the cobbles and, proudly conscious of its London counterpart, it lay at the very heart of an older, more insular Petworth.

TREAD LIGHTLY HERE

Arguably the earliest surviving photograph of East Street, dating perhaps from the late 1870s. *Mr. G. C. Ayling, Chichester.*

# 5

## EAST STREET

IT IS East Street's burden to carry the traffic that comes south from North Street. A little will go straight over at the Red Lion crossroads and some will turn left into Angel Street to travel eastward but most will turn right to continue a journey southward. The one-way system of course spares East Street the traffic going north and east on the return journey. Where Lombard Street seems to have become something of a backwater because of its alienation from the motor car, East Street, like North Street, gives above all a feeling of passage, while on-street parking on the west side at once enforces single-line traffic and slows that single line down. Has anyone ever seen a car overtake in East Street? Perhaps of all Petworth streets East Street gives the greatest consciousness of the traffic. In September 1670 the manorial court presented one Edward Tupper for laying luggs in the highway in the East Street of the town of Petworth to the danger of all persons travelling in the same street (PHA 3955). Luggs are poles or quite simply tree limbs. Unpopular as Master Tupper might have been with the authorities then, he would, one suspects, be rather more so today.

Most Petworth people were frequent visitors to East Street until the "new" Post Office closed in the summer of 1989. With only the sorting office now left, East Street may lack a little of its old drawing power but the archetypal Petworth town walk still remains the old town crier's beat: Market Square, New Street, East Street, Church Street, down Lombard Street and back into the Market Square. The new Post Office, as some still called it, was built just before the Great War and there are those who remember it in building, just as there are those who remember the old Post Office in the Market Square. East Street runs parallel with Lombard Street, back to back with illogical, irregular, very private gardens running between, a kind of lost world in the very centre of Petworth. The census returns tend not to treat East Street as a single entity, dividing it east and west and apportioning each side to a different enumerator. In truth the two sides are historically a little dissimilar, smaller houses and a cluster of shops on the west side, large private houses on the east. In the nineteenth century East Street, or at least its east side, was very much home to Petworth's doctors and professional men. East Street has never been a Leconfield Estate stronghold and one might expect to find rather less in Petworth House deeds regarding its history than one would other Petworth streets.

The census returns logically enough begin with George House, at the turn of the present century Dr. Beachcroft's private house and surgery. The entrance to the old surgery was by the coach-house to the left, the first window of George House being the waiting-room and the second Dr. Beachcroft's surgery. The bottle shed lay across the yard at the back. Doctors then employed their own dispensers and prescriptions were made up on the premises. *Tales of Old Petworth* (p. 92) talks of "a house now pulled down on the site of which the coach house and stables of Mr. Shout's, now Dr. Macdermott's residence, now stand." Its last tenant had been John Stedman the shoemaker. Dr. Augustus Shout appears in the 1871 census but Dr. Robert Wilmot in 1881. For two decades before, the house seems to have been home to the resident C.O. of the Rifle Volunteers, Petworth's nineteenth century equivalent of a Territorial Army unit. Major W. R. Barnes appears in the 1861 census. Major Arthur Knox late Life Guards in 1851. The house, formerly an inn called the George, had been rebuilt at the turn of the nineteenth century and is advertised in 1805 as "a handsome sash-fronted freehold messuage near the church . . . large and recently built" (Beck, *Inns* p. 137). The house was sold to the Earl of Egremont in 1812.

The George Inn was certainly well established by the early seventeenth century: an agreement (PHA Deeds OG 15/1) between the Earl of Northumberland and the people of Petworth concerning the water supply, speaks of a conduit "at the North End of South Street . . . over against a common inn there called the George". South Street can of course mean High Street as well as East Street but there can be no confusion here. Inventories for the George survive from 1672 and 1674. In 1672 there were fifteen rooms including specific painted chambers named as the Half Moon, Anchor, Flower de Luce, Crown, Bull and Cross Keys. Geoffrey Dawtrey's inventory of 1674 adds the Dolphin and the "Hostlers" but omits the Bull and Cross Keys. The inn would cease operating by the late eighteenth century and it is thought that only the cellars of the present house survive from the original George. There is no indication of what the inn looked like, other than as Miss Beck says, the suggestion in the inventories of a courtyard.

Adjoining George House to the south is the red brick "Institute" now an antique shop and not over the last century much used as a private residence. St. Mary's Church Magazine for January 1890 reports that it had been "lately occupied by Mr. H. T. Upton" but that Lord Leconfield now proposed transferring the Petworth Institute thither from the Town Hall. The Institute, in Arnold's words (*History* p. 94), incorporated "a Subscription Reading Society and a Working Men's Institute". For the move from the Town Hall the house in East Street was to be enlarged and adapted. The Parish Magazine reports that there would be several good rooms "for reading, for games, for a library and all the objects an Institute can require". The Institute seems to have been the particular preserve of Thomas Seward, a member of the Market Square ironmonger family, who had begun an "Albert Institute" in the upstairs rooms of what is now Austens in the mid 1860s. It would in the course of time merge, probably with an already existing subscription library, and move to the Town Hall. This change is not documented at present but may well be connected with alterations made by Lord Leconfield in the lower part of the Town Hall. Thomas Seward's Albert Institute was a force in further education for young working men and would continue so over the years.

An outspoken liberal in his social views, Seward was at the same time an equally outspoken High Churchman, an uncomfortable combination in the sequestered atmosphere of late nineteenth century Petworth. "I believe the time will come when the Powers that be in Petworth will have to provide a Free Library and Classes for continued education for the poorer classes and at the ratepayers' expense. We know very well how reluctantly our Authorities provide the Education the poor now get, but fortunately an enlightened Parliament has enforced it and may now enforce the reforms I now advocate". So Seward states in a manifesto announcing his withdrawal from an election for Honorary Secretary of the Institute in 1890 or 1891. The Evangelical Rector of the time, Charles Holland had apparently threatened to resign as President of the Institute if Seward were elected Secretary. It does not seem to have been Seward's radical views so much as his high churchmanship which had led Charles Holland to this drastic step. Seward in his turn had few illusions as to the catastrophic domino effect Charles Holland's resignation might have on the Institute he had so long nurtured. "I have also been told that if I am elected several first-class members would also leave: that is possible for the rich doing any particular act are sure to find imitators by certain minds among the smaller fry . . . pressure might even be brought so that the Rooms may be taken from us". The last clause would suggest opposition from the House itself and there are clear hints in the manifesto that this was not the first time Seward had encountered opposition from such a quarter.

The controversy seems in fact to reflect visits of the church missioner Mr. Wakeford to St. Mary's in 1890 and 1891, Mr. Wakeford's churchmanship being apparently to Seward's taste. "I feel so amply revenged, when the very opinions I was condemned for go forth from a pulpit in which had been preached such contrary doctrine." Thomas Seward was to die suddenly on a visit to Billingshurst in the following year, but his uncomfortable voice, now so long stilled, represents perhaps rather more than a storm echoing round a late Victorian tea-cup. He was the author of a book of religious poems of which I have never seen a copy, and editor too of a broadsheet called the Petworth Echo, apparently giving Institute news. As with the poems, no copy of this is known to survive and the discovery of either the poems or the broadsheet would be an important find. Thomas Seward had at his death amassed a museum and a library of several thousand volumes. The Institute would continue in various forms for generations but eventually fade away. It is probable that with the departure of Thomas Seward much of its crusading spirit departed too.

The old Girls' School, separated by cottages from the Institute, is now a private house. Sometime an Independent chapel the empty premises had been purchased by Lord Leconfield who "at his sole

Thomas Seward about 1885. Note the "Petworth Echo" at the foot of the table. *Photograph by Walter Kevis. Garland Collection.*

expense converted it into the commodious school, in which the girls are at present instructed". So wrote Arnold in 1864. Long the realm of Miss Elson, the turn of the century Girls' School was famous for its entertainments even if the intrepid headmistress was not always as punctilious about applying for a licence to stage them as Lord Leconfield's agent would have wished. The Girls' School would continue long after Miss Elson retired and was for a generation under Miss Wootton's charge. There are many who will recall it as a school and some who remember that day in 1942 when the bomb fell on the Boys' School and the colour drained from the teacher's face as a messenger whispered the first inklings of the tragedy. In the 1950s the premises doubled on Thursday evenings as a home for St. Mary's Youth Fellowship, the large hall being equally suitable for skittle-ball and ballroom dancing — if at different times! The classrooms were ideal for "beetle-drives", more popular then than now perhaps.

The 1724 sketch-map shows two houses occupying the area from the old Girls' School to the former Boxall House. One is Henry Martin's and the more southerly Thomas Winter's "next the street". It was a large house let in three tenements for £8 a year. The present cottages are more modern, and are now a little retired from the road. "Thomas Arnop's house and yard" is without question Boxall House, now an antique shop. At the close of the last century it was the home of Miss Emma Blagden who lived there in some style with servants and a large garden. The census records suggest that her bachelor uncle John Blagden the surgeon had occupied the house before her. The large garden which was so much a feature of the house survived until the late 1980s when, like so many Petworth gardens before it, it fell prey to the developer. Even if the current craze for infilling is a temporary one, its effect on Petworth as a town of unexpected gardens will endure. Garden land once taken does not readily revert to its former use. Deeds suggest Richard Stokes sub-seneschal of the manor as an early seventeenth century occupant of this house, while Thomas Arnop, master of the workhouse, held the house a century later. His will of 1737 disposes of several different Petworth properties let out to tenants but unfortunately does not specify them in detail. The old name Boxall House does not go back before this century, referring to a contemporary owner Mr. Boxall the builder. He is remembered as bringing his car out into East Street from the entrance to the east, a manoeuvre which would of course have seemed far less intrepid between the wars than it would now. The house has never, until the last decade, been used as shop premises.

Boles House sequestered behind the high wall is new, built on a part of what was in 1724 "Mr. Cook's garden" i.e. the garden of the adjoining Stringer's Hall. The construction of this latter building, now divided, but clearly a single entity in 1724, is generally attributed to Richard Stringer, son of Richard Stringer the mercer from Pettifers in Church Street. The younger Richard Stringer, like his father before him, was a wealthy man and his will leaves among other property his "great houses" in Back Street and Church Stile Street, Back Street confusingly being an old name for East Street. The beneficiaries are his great nephews John and Richard Cook. The "great houses" are almost certainly Stringer's Hall and Pettifers. The date 1654 and the initials R.S. at the top of a rain-water pipe on the building's north side are usually, and doubtless correctly, taken to corroborate Stringer's involvement in the construction of Stringer's Hall, but it may be that he incorporated parts of an earlier Elizabethan building into his new house. Eighteenth century information on this important house is decidedly sketchy: the 1724 reference to Mr. Cook's house establishes the Cook family as still holding the property at this time but by 1762 a Mr. Burnett returns sixty windows for tax purposes, presumably for the still undivided building. A notable occupant in the early decades of the nineteenth century was William Tyler, legal agent to the Third Earl of Egremont and after his death in 1835 the house would remain in the hands of the Gould family, William Tyler's sister and her descendants for many years, the last Miss Gould dying at Stringer's Hall in the late 1930s. The building had at this time long been partitioned; so large a house no doubt being difficult to maintain even in a period when domestic help was readily available and affordable. "At one time," writes Dr. Brydone, looking back to the mid-nineteenth century, "Stringer's Hall was let to Dr. Turner, and his partner, Dr. Morris lived at the back." Dr. Morris was to remain in East Street for some years, and his two sons were to become eminent surgeons, Sir Henry Morris once returning to Petworth to attend Lord Leconfield personally. Parts of the house seem to have been empty at the outbreak of war in 1914. There are stories of timber from the staircases being ripped away and used for fuel. The long sojourn of the Gould family may have led, as such sojourns often do, to a certain decay. Dr. Brydone has a curious tale which he leaves floating timelessly in the air: if it has perhaps gained a little in the telling it does suggest a certain stagnation:

> "Mr. Gould was a great collector of all and everything. He had a room packed with really good furniture but made no use of it. Once he invited the Rector to see his treasures but when he unlocked the door there was nothing to be seen but a thick fog, but old Mr. Gould waved his arms and cleared away the thick grey cobwebs that had formed the curtain of fog. Alas! When he died and there was a sale most of the furniture was rotten with worm. Amongst his 'collections' was a skeleton and hundreds of empty match boxes."

The square building in the lane has a history that is doubtless unrivalled by any similarly unpretentious building in the town but which leaves us with an almost impossible task of sifting fact from legend. According to Dr. Brydone, "they say" that the strongly barred windows and stout construction of the building are the remains of William Tyler's office and were originally intended as a preventive against the attentions of the mob. "They say" always indicates a certain unease on the doctor's part — a brush with the apocryphal — but certainly William Tyler appears to have had enemies among the ordinary people, even if the tradition that when he died they filled his grave with cabbage stumps and danced on it can be discounted as a later fabrication. Dr. Brydone knows too another tradition that thieves came to the office one night in 1810 and stole the money kept there to pay the Estate wages. It was rumoured that they had come up an underground passage from the Hermitage summer house, but the story does not stand or fall on this. An allied memory is found in some handwritten notes made by an unnamed occupant of the Hermitage in the 1920s. This claims that the building "became a pay house for agricultural labourers and the story goes that £200 was deposited upon a table in the room and the attendant absented himself for a few minutes and an early bird pinched the money bag for keeps".

Whatever the truth of this, and there may well be a kernel of truth somewhere, William Tyler's unpopularity was legendary. By virtue of his position as agent to the Earl of Egremont, Tyler clearly bore the brunt of the agricultural discontent of the early nineteenth century but he does not appear to have tried in any way to come to terms with this. His unilateral and high-handed decisions to lower estate wages alarmed Mr. Upton, clerk of the works. It was an expedient Tyler had tried in 1823 with a conspicuous lack of success and Upton was understandably chary of a renewed attempt a few years later. At the very least, as he pointed out, skilled men would leave the Earl's employ and go to someone who paid the normal rate. At this distance in time it is difficult to say why Tyler so especially incurred, almost courted, the people's displeasure. Indeed for a man whose signature adorns a myriad documents of the period and whose name appears wherever one looks at Petworth in the first decades of the last century, Tyler remains a curiously remote and unknowable figure. His nephew Thomas Gould, writing from abroad to a younger brother in 1826, and reflecting on earlier days spent in the office, writes of his uncle: "You must consider the multiplicity of his business, the importance of which keeps his mind constantly employed and leaves him little leisure to attend to every frivolous affair that may occur among his servants." (O & A uncatalogued material, box 49). John Osborn Greenfield (*Tales*, p. 44) had no doubts as to the rancour Tyler aroused among certain elements in the Town:

> "To parade the effigies of men who had given offence was then a frequent practice in Petworth. I have seen our late Rector Sockett and afterwards Tyler and his man Goatcher thus exhibited. Once in Tyler's latter time they were thus carried about at Egdean Fair on September 4th. Haslett and others hired a tramp with stentorian lungs and his woman to sing obscene songs about Tyler to such a degree offensive that no lady could venture to come into Petworth, nor any female of responsibility, show her face in the streets. For these songs were roared out day and night from many mouths, not only in the town but in every tap room also. The fellow was called 'Bandy'".

Or again Greenfield (p. 66) speaks of the "Tyler" riots in which Charles Herrington played so prominent a part and "for which he was tried at Horsham and got a long term of imprisonment". Greenfield's account suggests rioting on a large scale but in fact the Assize records preserved at the Public Record Office throw a rather different light on matters. The case was tried at Lewes and not at Horsham and seems more of an isolated act of defiance than a general disturbance even if it is clear that Herrington had a good deal of public support. The original summons mentions four men, Charles Herrington, carpenter, William Vinson, carpenter, David Cloudsley otherwise Sharp, labourer, and Edward Meachen, labourer. Charles Herrington is clearly the instigator and seen by the authorities as such; of the others, Meachen and Vinson were in their twenties, Cloudsley is not otherwise known. Herrington was already in his early forties, with previous convictions for assault in 1810, 1815 and 1820.

The original indictment survives in the Public Record Office (PRO ASSI 35/274/4 4636) and accuses Herrington and his accomplices of making a gibbet and gallows and an effigy intended to represent William Tyler, with words placed on the hat saying "Iniquity Rewarded" and a cloth on the breast with the words "a preventive to the corruption of youth". They had made too another effigy representing a person not at present identifiable by the jurors and placed on that a placard saying "Jackal the Bulldog's provider". These figures were then suspended on the gibbet and gallows and carried "in through and along divers public streets and highways at or near Petworth aforesaid and also before and near the dwelling house of the said William Tyler" and many other houses besides in such a way as to suggest that Tyler had been guilty of some capital offence. The indictment carries a second and allied count, i.e. of defaming Tyler.

Herrington, clearly conceived as the ringleader, was imprisoned for a year, and bound over on his provision of two separate sureties of £40 "to keep the peace and be of good behaviour toward all His Majesty's subjects especially toward William Tyler the prosecutor for two years more to be computed from the expiration of the said one year.". The other three defendants received one month's prison each. The incident seems a little obscure and will probably remain so: the case makes no mention of any justification they may have had for their behaviour. We could wish Master Greenfield had told us a little more. Herrington died in 1854 but Vinson and Meachen were both to die young, in 1836 and 1839 respectively.

The Hermitage away to the east is, says the anonymous writer from the 1920s, "a Regency Cottage of interest", added to in about 1880 to provide a large bedroom, dressing room and four rooms below. For a while in the mid-nineteenth century it was home to Alexander Combes, Chaplain at Petworth Gaol but over the whole period is most closely connected with the Gould family. The summer house and bowling alley make it a unique Petworth property. Although it fell into some disrepair in the 1970s it has survived with much of its old distinction. Its remote aspect has given rise to much talk of a monastery being here in pre-reformation times but no real evidence of this has ever come to light. I am inclined to think that the idea arises from a misinterpretation of certain pre-reformation wills where there is mention of the Brotherhood of Corpus Christi. This was not a fraternity of monks but a lay society who were pledged to assist at services and see among other things that proper obsequies and remembrances were carried out for the souls of the departed.

The name Daintrey House reflects the long occupation of the Daintrey family from the mid-nineteenth century but the house is obviously far older. An earlier occupant had been James Goble who declared forty-two windows in the 1762 Window Tax Return. A glance however from a suitable vantage-point in the Bartons shows that while the brick façade at the front is relatively late, the timber-framed back has Elizabethan features. Mrs. Barnes draws attention to a handsome ceiling decorated with festoons of flowers in stucco. Nairn saw Daintrey House as the most ambitious building in Petworth "a chequerboard of grey and red brick". He liked too the marvellous iron railings separating the front garden from the pavement. J. O. Greenfield (*Tales* p. 92) attributes the building of the new front to William Stoveld, the banker and says that he styled the house "My Manchen" after the Mansion House in London. Actually *Tales* personifies the house as "Mr. Manchen" but colourful as this is, I think it may be a misprint. According to Greenfield Mr. Row had his ironmonger's shop here before he moved to Market Square and the house had originally belonged to Mr. Falkner a draper, presumably that same Benjamin Falconer who at one time had his premises on the site of Eagers in the Market Square. When New Street did not exist and Trump Alley was a recognised thoroughfare, East Street and Market Square would have lived far more closely together than they do now.

William Stoveld took over a bank in Market Square, first started by William Upton, but seems also to have been something of an entrepreneur. PHA 78 reflects an exchange of letters between the Rev. John Peachey and the Third Earl of Egremont concerning a boxing match to be held at Northchapel in the autumn of 1828 "an entertainment to be given by Mr. Stoveld". The Earl, while no great enthusiast for pugilism, does not place himself under the abolitionist banner of Mr. Peachey, drawing instead a studious distinction between boxing and fighting: "I believe that this prejudice against boxing arises from a confusion of terms, for although boys and blackguards in anger *fight* with their fists and are therefore guilty of an unchristian feeling, yet those men by their strength in good humour, box, but do not *fight*, because they have no unchristian feeling towards each other . . ." The Earl decides that he will not use his authority to stop the proposed contest, even assuming that he has the power to do so, and of that he has some doubt.

In the autumn of 1830 a letter was found in the porch at Daintrey House. It began, "Gentlemen take care of your cattle and yourselves for we are resolved to burn down the house of Mr. S. and perhaps the whole of Petworth . . .". It was the time when the so-called Swing Riots were sweeping through Sussex and this was just the type of anonymous threatening letter in which the Swing organisers specialised. As bankers, the Stovelds would, of all people, represent privilege and capital while the boxing match in 1828 hardly suggests that the family kept a low profile. The writing of the letter would much later be attributed to Sarah Mitchell, a servant girl working in the Stoveld household. She had, she said, been told to write the letter by one John Morley, "a tall dark stranger" from London she had first met in Back Street. He had asked her also to set fire to her master's house and given her an incendiary device, a ball which could be broken, dampened and then left to combust of itself within the hour. She had met him again in New Street a little later and he had asked her if she had set the house on fire. She replied that she had never actually agreed to do so. It was only when her mistress scolded her on Petworth Fair Day that she went up into the loft over the stable and tossed the ball among a pile of hoop-chips. The resulting fire was soon put out.

Mary Laurence, another servant, said that she too had been accosted by a stranger on two occasions before the letter was found and had been asked if she were a servant to Stoveld the banker and which house his was. Adding to her statement Sarah Mitchell recalled another meeting with John Morley on a Sunday afternoon. She had walked with him from the Angel in the direction of Byworth when she was supposed to be in church. The Stovelds did not press charges but Sarah was given a year's hard labour for having on her own admission written the letter. The mysterious John Morley simply fades into history. (For a fuller account see the article by Trudy Foley in *Petworth Society Bulletin* No. 22.)

For much of the nineteenth century the house was home to the Daintrey family, Arthur Daintrey the solicitor and then his son C. J. Daintrey. On the latter's removal from Petworth in the early 1890s his sisters lived on in the house for many years. Ena Lee recalls looking out of the upstairs room at the Clock House in Church Street long before the Great War to see the sisters coming up from East Street to church, stately as galleons in their old-fashioned bustles. The two sisters were quite dissimilar. Miss Constance (Con.) was a well-known artist, while Miss Alice had charge of the Bailliewick farm on the way to Byworth. At one time the Daintreys had had the use of the High Street Club Room as a studio. The Bailliewick farm was operated virtually single-handedly by Mr. Tom Courtnay and was a really labour-intensive farm of the old kind. Tom Courtnay is remembered as taking milk up to the Cottage Hospital using a wooden yoke. In the *Petworth Society Bulletin* No. 48 Mrs. Gumbrell recalls life at Daintrey House in the early century . . .

> My sister, later Mrs. Shoubridge, worked for the Daintreys as a cook at Daintrey House. Miss Con. and Miss Alice who lived there were the sisters of Mr. Daintrey, at one time a solicitor in the town. Miss

Con. was an artist of some ability and spent a good deal of time abroad working on her art. Quite a few pictures of hers survive locally, some of local scenes but many of places on the continent. Miss Alice kept a stern eye on the farm. She was a hardy lady who always had a cold bath before breakfast, sitting in a saucer bath, shaped like a big saucer which she kept under the bed. The maid would bring up the cold water, then empty the bath when Miss Alice had finished with it. The domestic staff consisted only of the cook and the maid. When my sister was the undermaid she used to wait table. The cook made a butter cake and was told she could make herself a dripping cake. The cook however made herself a butter cake. When Miss Alice saw the cake she said, "That dripping cake really does look nice, we'll have that in the dining-room". Cook had to set to pretty quickly to make a proper dripping cake. If she'd let the other cake go into the dining room Miss Alice would have known it hadn't been made with dripping. The servants had to be in at eight o'clock and were allowed out Sunday afternoons provided they weren't "pleasuring" as Miss Alice put it. Miss Alice herself went to church every morning.

The present "Quest" premises on the corner junction with New Street were for generations Knights the Grocers, Mrs. Gordon Knight running the shop herself after the early death of her husband. The site is marked as a house and yard on a sketch made apparently as part of the Earl of Egremont's conveyance when New Street was about to be driven through the mass of gardens, houses and outhouses that preceded it. The Burgess family were very much connected with this site in the late eighteenth and early nineteenth century, Clement Burgess being described in Pigot's 1826 Directory as an "architect and stone mason". His yard was in the middle of the present road between Quest and the Red Lion. It is difficult to imagine now how different this part of East Street would have been when New Street did not exist, and the continuation with Middle Street was broken only by the junction with Angel Street. The Burgess home and premises would not have been a corner site at all, while Trump Alley to an extent performed the function of present-day New Street.

According to Brenda Knight, it was her grandfather James Loten Knight who first made the corner premises into a shop. In the

*Petworth Society Bulletin* No. 27 she gives a vivid account of this old-fashioned grocers in the period before 1914 . . .

> There were several grocers in Petworth then, the International Stores, still in New Street at that time, Greens in Church Street, Otways where the International Stores are now and of course Olders (now Portobello). With so much competition, friendly as it was, we had to be quite price-conscious. We were noted for our provisions, especially bacon even if we no longer smoked it ourselves. Butter we kept in the cellar and like most things it had to be packaged by us from bulk. We would try to package up in advance, or at least do so much in advance and leave some loose, handy to package if we needed it. We ground our own coffee at this time and I still have a mahogany chest of drawers lined with blue paper that was used for storing sugar. How the wasps used to like that chest of drawers! We did some greengrocery too — there wasn't the variety we have now and some things like oranges were only then in season around Christmas. We sold the usual things like cabbages, carrots, cauliflowers and even celery, but for the last my mother would never use the shop celery but always send one of us children up to the Misses Pullen at Egdean. Their father was an expert grower of celery. There were already some meats like tongue which came in cans and dried vegetables like butter beans which you would put into the bag with a small scoop. Mother got to know of a firm called S. and W. who did very high quality tinned fruit, pears, peaches, even things like figs. I particularly remember their "long branch" pineapple which was cut in long rectangles. In those days a firm like S. and W. would only let one grocer in the town have their goods and our link with S. and W. gave us a definite advantage in this field. I don't know whether the tinned fruit was delivered direct or came up from the station — goods might come either way. Only the coming of the first war ended our link with S. and W.
>
> The Audit Dinner at Petworth House was a major function and the order was carefully shared out among the various tradespeople. We always supplied the cheddar cheese. No ordinary cheddar though — we ordered it from Warren and Reynolds and the traveller would go and choose the cheese himself. What was left my mother sold in the shop and there was never any shortage of customers for it. It was agreed to be the best cheese ever seen in Petworth! . . .

Trump Alley still survives both as a name and an entity, although much of its significance disappeared with the building of New Street at the beginning of the nineteenth century. Up to that time it afforded a passage into Market Square without a long detour round High Street. In September 1672 the Manorial Court declared that "Mr. Thomas Mitchell, his heirs and assigns, have free liberty of egress, ingress and regress at all times with carts and carriages through the passage or gate leading from the East Street in Petworth and adjoining to the Little White Hart there unto the tenements of the said Thomas . . ." It had, they said, been an ancient way "time out of mind" (PHA 3955). The White Hart Tavern presumably fronted on to the alley and indeed Trump Alley is sometimes referred to as White Hart Lane in old documents. Henry Goble held this inn with the adjacent Great White Hart to the west during the mid-seventeenth century, his son John's widow being directed to sell the Little White Hart in 1696 to clear John's debts and legacies. (Original Will and Beck, *Inns* p. 140). Trump Alley is marked as an archaic name on the 1882 survey map but it is not clear what the origin of the name is. The cobbled remains of it are still to be seen in the garden of David's in Market Square. In later years a popular but unofficial name was "Blood Alley" a dubious tribute to the slaughter houses that huddled together in the lane.

The double-fronted shop on the other side of the alley, latterly a restaurant, would appear to have housed the old-established firm of Hiltons the Drapers, operating in East Street for several decades through the mid and late nineteenth century. A note in the *West Sussex Standard* of 25th January 1892 records the passing of Thomas Hilton at the age of 86. "He had been in business in Petworth for 60 years and had been a deacon and trustee of the Congregational Chapel for more than 25 years." No very early photograph of this part of East Street is known to survive but later pictures show Denmans as having the shop just before the Great War with the legend "Cabinet Maker and Upholsterer" above one window and "Dressmaker and Milliner" above the other. It is possible that Denmans had partly carried on the Hilton drapery tradition but equally possible that there had been some kind of interregnum. The shop to the north of Denmans looks much less established, more of a

The "new" Post Office in East Street in the late 1920s. Mr. Palmer the town crier and a certain degree of Garland affectation. *Photograph by George Garland. Garland collection.*

private house window enlarged to provide shop premises and showing only the beginnings of the present shop window. Denmans would later of course move to Norman Place and concentrate on restoring and selling antiques. The shop they vacated would be for generations Petworth Dairy, still well remembered for their morning coffee and lunches.

The 1882 Survey, usually such an important source, is remarkably reticent about East Street, paying most attention to the north-west corner and ignoring much of the rest of the street. It does however mark in a premises roughly in the position of the present Scrump Cottage as "the Curriers," italic capitals indicating an archaic name. The use of the definite article may well indicate the site of a curriers rather than a single place name and it may be that leather was once cured and dressed here. If so, nothing is at present known of this and it is not possible to pick up such a trade in Pigot's 1826 Directory. The Ordnance Survey Map of 1874 shows gardens extending northward over the site of what would later be the Post Office, but there may well have been previous settlement here. Miss Beck would have John Osborn Greenfield renting a house from the Leconfield Estate in this area about 1855 and Treswell's map, while not easy to interpret, seems to show a fair-sized property in this position in 1610. If a currier indeed worked here there may be some connection with the long-established tannery at Norman Place: the two trades are clearly allied.

On the other side of the Post Office lies what is effectively a small arcade of shops, originally three but now split and subdivided on the southern side of the Norman Place entrance. The northern part of the present building was still a private house in 1900, with the southern part attractively covered in creeper. It was to here that Bryants the stationers had moved from Church Street in the 1870s and Alice Bryant would have the shop for several decades. Talking of the early century Ena Lee recalls: "Miss Bryant's dear little shop which had lovely writing paper, postcards, Valentines and drawing paper. I loved to get in there." (*Petworth Society Magazine* No. 59.) Ena also liked Mrs. Burnett's toy and fancy goods shop on the farther side of the Norman Place entrance. This was a real treasure-house. "Berlin wool and Scotch Fingery, Claremont and

Peacock knitting yarns, baskets and bassinnettes" are all advertised in the Parish Magazine for March 1889. For Christmas 1900 Mrs. Burnett claims the best selection of cards and presents in the town, a speciality being Christmas cards and calendars with local views — "from a penny upward". A picture of the interior shows a mass of assorted cartons and a notice saying "Agency for servants".

The earliest extant East Street photograph, taken about 1880, shows the pattern of shops much as it would be for generations, much in fact as it is today. The further shop, now the Covert, was traditionally a greengrocers, Websters, as the century turned, then Tom Collins' "refreshment rooms" as Kelly's 1918 Directory has it. Collins' were dairymen too and had a milk delivery. In later years Streeters had a radio and electrical shop here. The 1881 census places William Botting "gardener" roughly in this position and it may be that he started the greengrocery business, almost entirely home-grown in those days. Equally however if the shop were simply used as a lock-up, the census will omit the name of the occupant. Census returns, helpful as they are, are often quite difficult to interpret. There is no strong tradition of memory regarding this line of shops but in those more leisured days before East Street was besieged with cars, this distinctive little row formed something of a high street on its own.

Norman Place is marked on the 1724 sketch map as having recently been purchased by Charles Seymour, Duke of Somerset. It would have been old then and its half-timbered exterior would be much admired by Nairn writing over two centuries later. The map marks "Johnson the taylor's house" as roughly corresponding with the later Bryants and shows a barn to the rear. Norman Place has always had a large hinterland and this is clearly delineated as a tannery on the 1874 Ordnance Survey Map, with extensive outbuildings. The tannery may have been an old-established one, William Lucas appearing here in the census returns for 1841, 1851 and 1861, latterly as a master tanner employing two men and a boy, while the Edward Lucas mentioned as a tanner by Pigot in 1826 will probably take the tannery back to that time at least. By 1871 James Worsfold, perhaps the same man who appears as a glover in Kellys 1853 Directory, has taken the tannery and is described by Kelly in 1874 as "tanner and fellmonger". In later years James

Worsfold would work in close conjunction with his son, W. J. Worsfold who operated basically as a veterinary practitioner. It was a natural combination, W. J. Worsfold being able to bring back skins from the farms he served as part credit against his charge for services. W. J. Worsfold's ledger book for 1893-1894 survives and the business seems not long to have continued after this, although the ledger book offers no reason for its demise. Henry Streeter's livery stables were here by the century's end. The veterinary practice was a large one, embracing Northchapel and Lurgashall to the north, Sutton to the south, River, Lodsworth and Lickfold to the west and Fittleworth to the east. The list of farms reads like a gazetteer: Limbo, Lyttleton, Osiers, Rotherbridge, Palfrey, Battlehurst and Gownfold to name but a few.

The business was pragmatic enough to modern eyes, nothing exotic and almost exclusively agricultural, draughts and powders, liniments and lotions, cordials and potions, ringing bulls, docking horses, castrating pigs, rasping a horse's teeth. Dogs and cats are mentioned only very occasionally, attention from a vet being clearly the exception rather than the rule and very much of a luxury. Medicines might be left for collection at Norman Place but Mr. Worsfold often of course attended in person. For the more outlying farms a charge would be made for the journey in addition to an attendance charge. All in all it was a busy practice.

The remainder of East Street to the junction with Church Street is not particularly well-documented, while the bend in the road has over the years consistently foiled the eye of the camera. The 1882 map marks a property north west of the present Covert as Herods, but the name, fascinating as it is, strikes no chord at present. The property at the junction with Church Street is marked on the map as Moor Manor and it is here probably, rather than, as legend has it, the adjoining Pettifers, that the ancient town house of the Dawtreys stood. The 1882 map is, on the face of it, a very accurate one: if it is not, we have certainly so far found little enough with which to disagree. Whoever filled in the old names clearly knew much that we do not, much that is no doubt still hidden away among the deeds at Petworth House. The 1724 sketch map shows Widow Randel's house and garden much in the position of the Covert and to the north an extensive area of garden.

EAST STREET

Bryants in East Street about 1900.

The present Petworth Antiques Market was long of course SCATS and formerly Petworth Engineering Co. but before that it had been Maybanks the Coachbuilders, shown in at least a couple of turn of the century photographs. The earlier history of the distinctive columned building is not known and in fact the columns, purely ornamental it would seem, have now been removed. An older name for the adjoining house is Norworth, a combination of Northchapel and Petworth and coined by the Payne family earlier this century. The house has recently been converted to an Indian restaurant. These premises are anciently connected with Hallidays the drapers and some stray invoices relating to this business were found during alterations. Hallidays were already well-established by 1826 when Pigot lists them as "drapers and glovers". Benjamin Dawes would continue the drapery business for many years and the inference must be that the present Antiques Market premises were used as commercial premises. The shop on the very corner, now dealing in Persian carpets, was a private house in the early century, later of course it would be Meachens the greengrocers.

A handbill found in Norworth by Mrs. Foley announces a coming performance of the comedy "She Stoops to Conquer" on Tuesday April 26th 1791. The poster is much decayed and in parts illegible. Tickets are available at the Printers? or of Mr. Thornton at the theatre (see *Petworth Society Bulletin* No. 10). The poster is headed "Theatre Petworth". It would be tempting but extremely unwise to see here an explanation for the formerly ornate front of the present Antique Market. Troupes of players certainly appeared at Petworth from time to time, according to John Greenfield occasionally even being allowed to perform at the Town Hall (*Tales* p. 44). At a somewhat later date James Frances Morgan who died at Petworth in November 1857 was a noted travelling thespian. A note in the *West Sussex Gazette* for November 19th 1857 reviews the play "Still Waters Run Deep" and refers to "his (Morgan's) little place of entertainment," a doubtful description of our building. Morgan probably had the periodical hire of a small premises, moving round on a kind of circuit of the main West Sussex towns. He seems to have been a familiar figure in Petworth over the years. It is significant that the company are in Petworth at fair time; as a matter of commercial acumen players made it their business to coincide with fairs, races or public events when people would come into town from outside. The only known venue for Mr. Morgan and his players is the Angel Inn where in October 1857 Morgan had a "Bespeak" by the Loyal Angel Lodge of Oddfellows (*West Sussex Gazette* 29th October 1857). The fact is that we do not really know the earlier use of the present Petworth Antiques building any more than we know where Mr. Morgan had his "little house of entertainment".

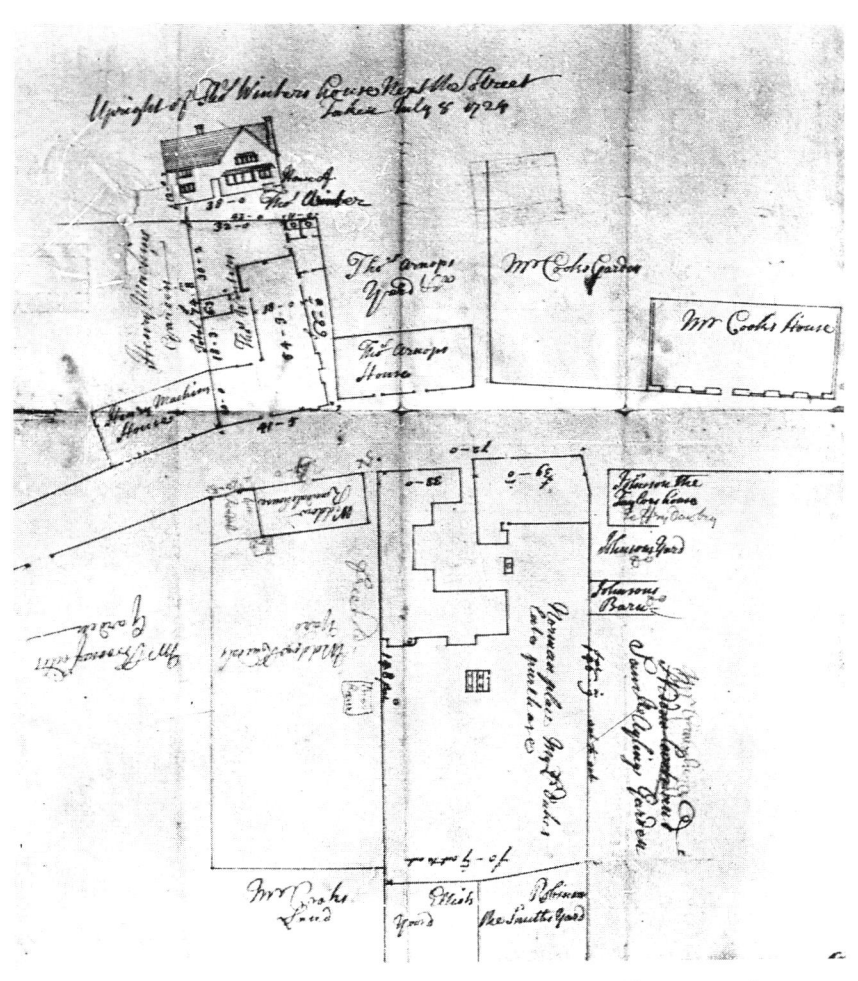

East Street in the 1720s. A sketch map. *The original is probably in Petworth House Archives.*

TREAD LIGHTLY HERE

Bartons Lane in the 1870s.

# 6

## BARTONS LANE

CHOKED as it invariably is with parked cars, Bartons Lane does not at first sight invite more than a questioning glance at the large wooden board displayed on the Coach House. We are at once warned against throwing stones, breaking lamps and other anti-social exuberances, and offered a reward of five shillings if we are able to "give such information as should lead to the conviction of every offender". Bartons Lane does however have revenge of a kind on the cars that choke it, for, ancient thoroughfare as it is, alone of the Petworth streets, it allows motor vehicles no passage through. For the pedestrian however, following the ancient wall on the left hand and rounding the corner where the breeze rustles the ivy, the fumes at the top of Church Hill become just a memory and there lie before him the green fields of Shimmings.

As an independent street name Bartons Lane may not in fact be very old although the name "Bartons" certainly goes back to a remote antiquity and the thoroughfare, for such it was, appears a relatively ancient one. An older name, prevalent at the turn of the century and later, but without perhaps ever gaining official recognition, is Craggs Lane, an oral usage falling now into disuse but still sometimes heard half-humorously on the lips of older people. For generations the lane had been the peculiar preserve of the Cragg family, painters, plumbers and glaziers, Wisteria Cottage long being the Cragg home, while their business premises lay at the end of the lane. The name Bartons has never been properly explained. While the word "barton" can mean a threshing floor, a farmyard or an estate farm, it is probably, as are so many of Petworth's ancient copyhold titles, in origin a family name. John Barton was a prominent figure in the rebuilding of Petworth House at the turn of the eighteenth century but the name Bartons can be traced back long before this time. Perhaps it owes its origin to one of John Barton's forbears.

Whilst the impeccable 1882 map gives Bartons as the ancient name for a property abutting on East Street immediately south of the old Girl's School, it is a curious anomaly that its extensive hinterland stretching away to the wall of the East Street Hermitage and the footpath that leads "Round the Hills" is more usually referred to as "the Bartons". The consistent and ancient use of the definite article is unexplained and may suggest that the idea of a family origin for the name is incorrect. The 1882 map declines to give the lane a specific name and in this concurs with the census returns from 1841 to 1881, which, ignoring the lane as an independent entity, have a tendency to treat Wisteria Cottage, then known as Parsonage Cottage, as the last house in North Street, or even, in 1841, as to the rear of Parsonage Lane! Parsonage Cottage in fact is one of those rare houses like William Guile's Corner House in Middle Street that receives an especial mention in the enumerator's instructions. It is almost as if the census officials felt this was just the kind of awkward anomalous property that if not carefully watched might somehow slither from their grasp altogether! More likely perhaps they simply found it a useful demarcation point.

While the census returns from 1841 onward are silent about Bartons Lane, the enumerator's instructions are clear enough about "The Bartons Gate by Gohanna", clearly implying that the old road from Bedham through the Gog Lodges and up into Petworth would come up by the Bartons and as at present out at the very top of North Street. The phrase looks back well beyond 1841 to a time years before when neither the present Shimmings Road nor the Fox Hill road from Petworth were yet in existence.

The Gog fields were in older days known as the Ideshurst or Hideshurst and there may in those days have been, as Lord Leconfield suggests (*Petworth Manor* p. 53), just a pathway with a stile over the glebe and into Petworth, i.e. nothing corresponding to the present Bartons Lane at all. In 1655 the way between Petworth and the Ideshurst became the subject of one of those leisurely disputes in the Court of Chancery that later ages find as enlightening as the original litigants no doubt found them expensive. The land as far as the brook and roughly to the present farmgate in the field beyond belonged to the Rectory Manor, while the Ideshurst fields sloping up from the gate belonged to the Earls of Northumberland. It would hardly be surprising if it had been the autocratic behaviour of Francis Cheynell, Presbyterian rector of Petworth under the Commonwealth, that sparked off the dispute, but its origins may in fact go further back. It was owing to the approved use of this route by two of the Earl's men and the dishonest behaviour of one of them that the Rector's barn had been burned down (Leconfield p. 53) and one of the Earl's witnesses, John Robson knows of a stoppage made some twelve years before "by one Mr. Skull in the time of Mr. Mountague late minister there by reason of some rudeness done by soldiers in the late troubles" — a rare reference to events at Petworth during the Civil War. Robert Ward however, testifying for the Rector and ninety years old in 1655, had left Petworth some thirty six years before and was positive that there had been no gate, and hence no way through, then. Looking back to the 1580s when Nicholas Smyth was parson, the Rector's lands had been so full of woods and bushes that there was no passage for a wain even if there had been a gate. Wood felled in the Ideshurst had to be brought out through Shimmings Lane (to the south of the present road).

The Earl's witnesses do not in principle differ from Robert Ward, looking basically to a gate being placed at the division of the two jurisdictions in the early 1620s, toward the end of the long ministry of Alexander Bownde or early in that of Richard Montague, at a time when the ninth Earl had been recently released from his long sojourn in the Tower. Nicholas Alderton from Shimmings had seen the Earl's servants go that way with carriages and the Earl himself travel that way with coaches and horses. John Hardham had been to school in Petworth and seen the servants of the Earl use the way "to go and choe horses and milke their cows". Playing at the Rectory as a boy when Mr. Bownde was minister, John Hardham particularly remembered one Bridger, the Earl's servant, driving his waggon through that way. John Underwood deposing on the Rector's behalf even remembered that when Mr. Mountague was rector, he had personally set up "a small whaple gate" for the Earl in the fence dividing the two grounds. The dispute seems to have rumbled on for a good while and Lord Leconfield mentions a second hearing in 1677. In the eighteenth century Charles Seymour, Duke of Somerset would establish his right of way by acquisition of the land once held by the Rectory Manor.

Treswell's 1610 map shows two fields just west of Shimmings as "Washing Leyes" and "Washing Lithe" respectively and these names appear to be connected with the cloth-making trade for which Petworth was noted in the mid-sixteenth century, as the contemporary traveller Leland observed in his Itinerary. The cloth industry is more particularly described by William Bullaker, deposing before the Chancery in 1592 in the dispute over enclosure and copyhold law between Henry Percy and his tenants (PHA 7362, CCP p. 35). Bullaker had been clerk to the estate surveyor in the reign of Queen Mary and looking back to the mid-century when he had lived in Petworth, recalled how the copyholders of the town, paying a set low annual sum for the copyholds they held of the Manor of Petworth, had used the money that accrued to them to dye and spin woollen cloth "and therewith sett the meane sort of tenants on worke" — to the obvious benefit of the community as a whole. It was, said Bullaker, the "racking" of the rents by Henry, the eighth Earl that had clawed the capital out of the cloth industry and effectively undermined it. He could honestly say that "he hathe seen of late that the greater number of the said copyholders are but in very bare and naked estate and carrye no countenance att all in respect what theire predecessors did".

Such evidence as there is, connects the Petworth cloth-makers with this area, as of course do the two field names on Treswell's map. A lease at Petworth House from 1590 recites how by the encouragement of Nicholas Smyth the Rector, William Mose the clothier had been to some considerable expense in building a house and store "in a parcel of glebeland called the Barton . . . for drying in fowle weather of kersyes". Kersey was a heavy, ribbed, type of cloth which appears to have been a Petworth speciality and the lease notes that the new drying shed had been "for the great benefitt and comon welthe of the towne of Petworthe".

The Bartons or at least "the Barton Ffield" is specifically mentioned, albeit incidentally, in a case brought before the Diocesan Court at Chichester in 1574 by one John Sucher of Petworth whose former betrothed Margaret Brown is no longer

The Bartons August 21st 1931. *Photograph by George Garland. Garland Collection.*

prepared to marry him as she had promised (*Petworth Society Bulletin* No. 57). From the present point of view there are two important points about the case: the clear connections with the cloth industry, and the mention of the Barton field. All the deponents whose occupations are given are intimately connected with the cloth trade. John Sucher's occupation does not appear; but Margaret Brown's mother kept house for William Mose the clothier and very likely the entrepreneur to whose initiative Petworth owed the Bartons drying shed. It has to be said that there are at least three generations of the Mose family all carrying the same Christian name, but while there may be some confusion between one generation and another, all seem to have had connections with Petworth clothmaking.

On a humbler plane Thomas Guye is a shearman (i.e. a shearer of woollen cloth) as is Thomas Gate. Nicholas Smythe is a capper, i.e. a maker of caps. The case turned on the question as to whether Margaret Brown had, as she claimed, made her promise of marriage conditional on gaining her mother's approval, or whether Nicholas Smythe the capper was correct in saying, "The contract was made betwene the said partyes without any condycon".

The reference to William Mose and the information that in face of her mother's disapproval "the same Margaret, perceyvinge that she cold not have her mother's good wyll, did appointe to mete with the said John in the Bartons Ffield at Petworthe afforesaid about ii howres before the goinge down of ye sonne" are certainly tenuous links but they do seem, with other hints like the location of William Mose's drying-shed, to place the cloth-making industry rather more in this rough area than in any other.

Whatever the ultimate fate of William Mose's shed, and he does seem to have embarked on his public-spirited enterprise at a time when the cloth-making trade in Petworth was in decline, it would appear that the Bartons field remained glebe. It was still glebe in September 1804 when the scholarly Rector of Petworth, Charles Dunster communicated to the Vestry Committee "his willingness gratuiously (sic) to accommodate the Parish with part of the Bartons (parcel of the Glebe) for an additional burying Ground". The Earl of Egremont as patron had signified his approbation (CVB p. 7). There was however first some doubt on the part of the Bishop of Chichester as to whether such a use of glebe land would be in order and Mr. Tyler, the Earl of Egremont's legal agent, was instructed to take counsel concerning this.

On 17th March 1805 the Vestry Committee informed Mr. Dunster that they would be pleased to accept his offer. Events then moved swiftly. The 30th June 1805 saw the appointment of a committee to consider "the expence of walling half an acre of ground out of the Bartons for making an additional Burial Ground". By the 4th July the Committee had considered and accepted John and Thomas Upton's estimate for enclosing the ground in question with a wall on the three sides that were at present unwalled and putting in a gate. There was a wall already on the south side forming a boundary with Mr. Tyler's property in East Street. A holly hedge stood on the northern side but after some deliberation this was removed and replaced with a stone wall. The new burial ground was consecrated on the 20th of October 1805, the very eve of Trafalgar although of course the Vestry Book makes no mention of this. Instead it notes that henceforth a fee would be chargeable for the indulgence of being buried in the old churchyard "because if it is permitted to all who may wish it the evil of a crowded burying ground will probably remain". A guinea therefore would be charged before any ground in the old churchyard could be broken up.

John Payne, parish overseer at Balls Cross, writes in his notebook for November 11th 1837 "at about 11 o'clock at night, George O'Bryan (sic) Earl of Egremont died, in the 86 year of his age and was buried in his vault in the Bartons. November 21st 1837. He was drawn to church by 12 men on a 4 wheel carriage erected for that purpose, and a great many people attended the funeral of his Lordship".

Backing on to the Bartons cemetery, now long disused, is Bartons Cottage, today a private house, but for so long the base of Craggs the plumbers, with Thayres the metal-workers to the side. Some tradition survives of Craggs at least in the period between the wars but there is at present no first-hand account of Thayres the smiths, only a number of turn of the century invoices. John Standing went to Craggs to work as a boy in the mid 1920s and was already half-conscious of a firm existing to an extent on tradition . . .

"Cragg and Son still carried one specialist painter, Charlie Denyer, but it was said that at one time Craggs had employed fifteen. They had decorated the rooms at Petworth House it was said. I don't know, but what they did have were a number of very high "strods", like enormous steps on which boards were laid to enable painters to work at ceilings or high walls. They were never used in my time. Another link with a distant past was the huge pole ladder, its sides formed from a single trunk split in half, and so long that it had to be laid through one outhouse, the Bartons Lane premises themselves, and out at the back. It was still used occasionally for premises like Eagers in Market Square, having to be hauled up on a rope thrown down from an upper bedroom window and attached on the ground: it was of course far too heavy to be simply lifted into position like a normal ladder. The poles were pretty solid but yes, it did bend alarmingly in the middle. Another venerable piece of equipment I did see used was the big old shepherd's hut that housed tools and equipment, towed down by lorry for a job in Station Road . . .

The Bartons Lane premises had work benches on the ground floor, used for knocking up lead and jobs like that, while in the left hand corner was a forge. Saturday mornings we might use it to make up or sharpen chisels. Upstairs was the paint shop and the glazing shop. Mr. Cragg had a diamond which he used to cut glass, no one else being allowed to use it. Craggs were glaziers too. I can see him now tapping the glass after he had cut it with the diamond. On the ceiling upstairs were pasted handbills of travelling shows that had come to Petworth, they would be of great interest now but no one bothered with such things. The paint shop had drawers with the different powders clearly marked with the colour, while on the wall, as you came down the stairs, were thick wodges of paint where over the years the painters had rubbed off their brushes. They looked like nothing so much as bunches of grapes, but were really multi-coloured knobs, big enough to hit with a hammer and showing all the different colours if you cut off a cross-section."

(*Petworth Society Magazine* No. 57)

Craggs was a multi-faceted business, responsible among many other things for Petworth's gas, the maintenance of the East Street obelisk being a particular concern; they were plumbers and workers in lead, glaziers, painters and well experts. They were even responsible to the Parish Council for the fire hoses, cleaning them after use and laying them out to dry in the Market Square like great white lines of spaghetti. When William Cragg retired the firm was taken over by the Sumersell brothers, Jack a member of the existing staff, and his brother Arthur who was an accomplished tinsmith. The latter craft, considerable as it was, was in decline by the early 1930s and Arthur, while retaining an interest in the firm, did not take an active part in later years.

Just up the lane was Francis Gaudrion Morgan's studio, an appendage to his chemist's shop in Church Street. Early photographs show it as a new-looking wooden building and it was probably purpose-built for Morgan, a remote forerunner of George Garland's wooden studio in Station Road. It is clearly marked "Studio" on contemporary maps. How long the building survived after Morgan retired to Brighton in the 1880s is not known but in later years the triangular strip of land was used for allotments. No one knows what became of Morgan's glass negatives, although many of his portraits survive as prints pasted on to card. Often the subject is unknown. A few Morgan views survive too but a very few. There is a tradition that the allotment site was popular because there were a lot of big sheets of glass about which were useful to make impromptu cloches. Had these sheets of glass once been Morgan's negatives? We shall never know and if this was indeed their fate it is better perhaps that we do not know.

TREAD LIGHTLY HERE

Angel Street February 11th 1932. *Photograph by George Garland. Garland Collection.*

# 7

## ANGEL STREET

ON FEBRUARY 2nd 1804 at four o'clock in the afternoon two strangers arrived at the Angel Inn riding on a single horse. They put the horse into the inn stables and came in for beer. William Muggeridge, assistant ostler at the inn, chatted to them for a while in the kitchen but on his declining to drink with them, one of the strangers became unpleasant and threatened to throw the beer in his face. The two men were clearly somewhat out of the ordinary and gave the impression that they were smugglers who had been up country with goods. The more assertive of the two went out into the town and returned carrying a long hunting-whip with a hammer handle. It was the kind of whip that would be used for driving several led horses, an odd purchase it would seem for two men who had only a single horse between them! The curious pair left about six in the evening, and a dark, dull rainy evening it was, paying Muggeridge for the horse feed and departing, as they had come, on the single horse. When their strange visitors were safely gone, the Angel kitchen was aflame with discussion. While some agreed the men were smugglers, others thought they were more likely to be horse-thieves and that news would soon come in of stolen horses.

They did not have to wait for long. William Baxell a licensed hawker and his family travelled the county "with a kind of horse waggon", keeping four horses to draw the waggon. On the 2nd of February Baxell had fed the horses and left them on Hampers Common. It was seven o'clock and darkness had long fallen. One horse had been fettered but on the next morning when he returned, the other three horses were missing; a black mare, a bay gelding and a bay mare pony. After searching the commons and lanes on the Friday, Baxell strongly suspected theft and, hearing of the singular pair seen on the Thursday evening at the Angel, set off westward in search of the thieves and his lost horses. Baxell's pursuit of his stolen horses, his piecing together of their progress by the accounts of turnpike men along the way, and his ultimate rediscovery of them, fifty-five miles westward at Sherfield Hatchet near the Wiltshire border need not concern us here (see *Petworth Society Bulletin* No. 17 and PHA 6315-6). The two men were Richard Carter and Jethro Cheeseman, the latter, says his subsequent indictment, "perhaps the most daring and notorious of a gang of villains who have for several years past infested Sussex and the neighbouring counties by burglaries and felonies; and by horse stealing".

The first mention of the Angel Inn as such may come from 1799 when Somerset Lodge was auctioned there. Deeds go back to 1720, the property being conveyed as a public house to Thomas Hampton, formerly the lessee, in 1721. It is not certain that the inn was known as the Angel at this time. In former times it seems to have been the family house of the Trew family, well-known Petworth maltsters, and was always very closely connected with Garlands, the ancient copyhold on the opposite side of the street. Part of Garlands is now the Angel Shades, while a very old and picturesque building on part of the present car park was demolished in 1939. The name Angel as a title for public houses is not uncommon and the popular notion that the name is connected with lingering medieval traditions as to the healing properties of the nearby Virgin Mary Spring may perhaps owe as much to a later wistful recollection as it does to hard fact. The history of the building cannot effectively be traced back before the earliest surviving deed in 1720. The fact that it is not shown on Ralph Treswell's map of 1610 means only that since the Angel fell within the confines of the old Rectory Manor, it did not form a part of Treswell's survey. Clearly the present building, at least in part, predates Treswell.

By the early nineteenth century the Angel Inn was home base for Petworth's oldest and most prestigious Friendly Society. The "Old Blue", "Angel Blue", or "Society of Good Fellowship" as it was more formally known would remain at the Angel until it was eventually disbanded in 1910. No doubt it owed its origin and close links with the local gentry to a feeling among the latter that a local Friendly Society might be an important instrument of self-help and might ease the burden on the Poor Law legislation. Thomas Sockett the rector and the Mitford family from Pitshill gave the Society backing over many years, albeit at a certain distance. The foundation of the Old Blue seems to have taken place at the Half Moon Inn in the Market Square (see WSRO MP 1868) but when records begin in 1822 the Society has clearly been ensconced at the Angel for some years. Of the reason for leaving the Half Moon no hint now survives. The "Old Blue", perhaps because of its close links with the local gentry, appears to have been a particularly staid organisation of its kind, the main activity taking place on Whit Monday when there would be an Annual General Meeting and a dinner. Preceded by a band, the members, in the Old Blue's heyday well over two hundred, would march through the town to church in time for divine service before returning for a convivial dinner at three o'clock. A charge of two shillings was levied for the dinner and liquor and only members who were in receipt of relief from the Society would be excused. Best clothes would be worn and the blue sashes and rosettes of the Good Fellowship; no doubt there was a banner too.

The early years were probably fairly stable ones but, a generation on, the Old Blue would run into the kind of problems that sooner or later beset all independent societies of the kind: in brief, the founder members would grow old together and need succour from the "Club", younger members would fight shy of joining an ageing society and a great chasm would open up. It was a situation that would never resolve itself because it was effectively incapable of resolution. What the Old Blue lacked too were the convivial Club Nights so attractive to working men and so suspiciously viewed by clergy and gentry alike. It would pay a heavy penalty for its lack of appeal to prospective new members. Regular monthly committee meetings perused applications for relief and the minute books record these from 1822 to the Society's closure in 1910. After about 1845 the story of the Old Blue is of a Society run aground. The growth of the federated Societies like the Oddfellows (allowed to operate from the Angel by Mr. Jones the landlord in 1848, to the considerable chagrin of the resident Old Blue) and the Foresters effectively spelled the end for the Old Blue. Starved both of funds and new adherents it would die a long, lingering death (see *Petworth Society Bulletins* Nos. 41, 42, 43, 45, 47 and 53).

Perhaps the most famous landlord of the Angel was John Osborn Greenfield (1802-1869) author of the *Tales of Old Petworth*, reminiscences of early nineteenth century Petworth, annotated by an unidentified writer a good generation later. A single printed copy of Greenfield's recollections, used as an impromptu beer-mat at the Angel nearly forty years ago, was rescued by George Garland and was for many years the only known copy. Recently however the entire text has been discovered in the *West Sussex Times and Sussex Standard* for 1891 and 1892. This latter version has some additional matter, the end part of Garland's original beer-mat having apparently become detached and lost. The annotator was working as he writes himself "in the room in which Mr. Greenfield was, and I am at this present time, scribbling away" (*West Sussex Times*, 9th January 1892). John Osborn Greenfield, as his annotator reasonably enough points out, was "from the post that he occupied . . . more especially enabled to collect and report the sayings and doings of his contemporaries and their immediate ancestors." Curiously the Angel Inn does not figure very prominently in Greenfield's recollections, written, one would suppose, in a comfortable retirement, Mr. Jones managing the Angel for him. Direct recollection of life at the Angel is lacking, and there is nothing to match the vivid account of the arrival of the horse-thieves. Vivid Greenfield can certainly be, but he ranges rather over Petworth as a whole, beginning with the classic account of dinner at Mr. Garland's in Market Square at Christmas 1812, moving through such items as skimmingtons and rough music, travelling players and stage-coach rivalries, to the lore of the Smugglers' Lane, and then to the border of the supernatural with the adventures of old Sue Redding. For a vignette of Angel Street itself we may instead turn to a memory preserved in the Milton family and going well back into the nineteenth century. "In Angel Street there lived an old lady who had thirty cats, each with their own little chair and dish, with which they sat with her at table, napkins tied around each neck, and each with their own little bed, in neat rows in a bedroom!" (*Petworth Society Bulletin* No. 15). In later years the Angel Inn was advertised as a "Family and Commercial Hotel" and catered particularly for commercial travellers in those days when representatives travelled by train and bus and were long periods away from home.

Egremont Row, on the hill diagonally across the street from the Angel, was built for Lord Leconfield's workmen in the mid-nineteenth century. The story goes that Mr. Brydone, then his Lordship's land agent, exceeded the specification on the project and was dismissed. Certainly by Victorian labourers' standards the cottages have a certain opulence. The story has a strange twist: Brydone had been a family friend at the great house, and, despite his dismissal, so remained. He stayed on in Petworth and founded the Market Square solicitors' practice, later to be known as Brydone and Pitfield and still in business as Anderson, Longmore and Higham.

Perhaps the very first tenant of Egremont Row was Philip Hoad the Market Square boot-maker, the Lord Leconfield of the time wishing to demolish Hoad's Market Square cottage and shop. Philip Hoad had been thinking of retiring anyway. His youngest son Harry Hoad would take over the cottage years later. Harry Hoad was a wood carver of consummate skill and in later years restored some of the Grinling Gibbons carvings at Petworth House. His daughter Ethel's recollections of early century life in Egremont Row (*Petworth Society Bulletins* Nos. 45 and 50) conjure up a late Victorian and Edwardian world of careful husbandry in large gardens, beekeeping and fruit trees, oil lamps and candles, ratafia biscuits and ipecuanha wine. Various Leconfield Estate personnel moved in and out of Egremont Row in those years, as of course they have done ever since — a French chef, an Italian chef, Messrs. Smith and Lambert the real tennis professionals and many more. As virtually everywhere else in Petworth, soldiers were billeted in Egremont Row in 1915, four in the Hoad home and a number in the house next door which had been temporarily vacant. So many vowed they would return in peace-time to visit those who had looked after them so well: so few returned.

These three recollections from Ethel Place give a particularly vivid view of life at 353 Egremont Row in the years leading up to the 1914 war.

> On Christmas Eve all stockings were hung up at the foot of the bed but excitement kept us awake until at last mother called out to us, saying "If you don't keep quiet and go to sleep, you will find that Father Christmas has left nothing for you, I can hear his sleigh bells a little way off." So at last peace reigned until very early when we

groped in the darkness for our full stockings. There were always a few coppers and an orange, some sweets and a little white or pink sugar mouse in the foot and then our presents. About breakfast time the Town Band usually came round to play carols. We all then set to to help mother, for she had a busy time preparing Christmas dinner. Sometimes we had a turkey, sometimes a goose with bread sauce and various vegetables — followed by the plum pudding, alight with the whiskey which Dad poured over it from a hot tablespoon and lighted with a match. Boxing Day, instead of pudding we had a Snapdragon, for this mother had previously put raisins in water till they were big and soft. When they were well drained they were put on a big dish, which was placed within reach of us all, and then they were lighted as the Christmas pudding had been. Then full of laughter and fun we all snatched them out of the blue flames to eat, accompanied with nuts and fruit. When friends or neighbours greeted us they were regaled with a small glass of mum's cherry brandy or sloe gin and mince pies. Our Morrello cherries were lovely very big dark red with very small stone and full of juice quite different to the ones I've seen nowadays. Spirits were cheap then whisky 3/6 and gin 2/6 a bottle. We children had home made ginger beer, which too was jolly good. There was a cellar at 353 Egremont Row. One half was dark, where potatoes and other winter vegetables were stored, the other lighted half was where the wine was placed. Dad had a full set of brass handbells which he and the boys were good at playing so sometimes we had a litle concert at home and if the weather was too bad for Church going we would sit round the fire in the sitting room by the light of the four candles in their gilded sconces, which Dad had made and fixed on the wall, and sang our favourite hymns.

Mother made plenty of jams and pickles, also wines. The parsnip, dandelion and elderberry were especially good. The latter was flavoured with cloves and ginger and we always sampled it on Fair night, hot as a night cap. For heating the wine mother had a thing she called a pipkin. I think it was made of earthenware and had a short handle to hold it over the red hot coals and we children always had a nip before scampering off to bed. There was no loitering on cold nights for there was no gas or electric heating and often long icicles hanging outside from the roof, but mother had had hot bricks in the oven, then wrapped in a piece of flannel and put in our beds. The beds were wooden with a solid back board at head and

ANGEL STREET

Early century Shimmings. *Mr. C. Vincent.*

foot and wooden latts between, on which was laid a horse hair mattress and then a nice plump feather bed so we were soon snug and asleep.

A visitor we were always pleased to see was a man from the coast with his cartload of fish when there had been a huge catch of herrings and mackerel. He would ring a bell and the women would run out with their dishes. Herrings were 8 a 1/- and mackerel 5 a 1/- all sparkling and fresh. Mother had a sort of wire cage and when the herrings had been cleaned and washed she placed the fish between the two wire sides and fixed them together. This was then hung by its two hooks to the top bar of the open kitchen fire. It had a little tray at the bottom to catch the drips. When one side was cooked the cage was reversed. Herrings or bloaters were lovely.

In the early years of this century, all that land bordered by the path alongside the Roman Catholic Church and Angel Street itself belonged to the Upton family at Grays, called Meadow Lodge in the mid-Victorian census returns. All, that is, except for the little piece of ground outside the Roman Catholic Church which forms the very apex of the triangle; this belonged to the Daintrey family in East Street and was always light-heartedly known to the Upton family as Daintrey Park.

The Upton family had a very considerable influence on this part of the northern side of Angel Street: Hill Cottage belonged to the family and was rented for a time by Mr. Pitfield the solicitor. The Barn was put together from four old cottages on the site. Mitchell "Mike" Upton lived in what is now the Cottage and dealt in batteries and radios — he had been trained in the new electrics at Ferranti in London at the turn of the century. He had a counter just inside the front door and a generator in the garage at the back. Arnop's Leith was built on the builder's yard toward the top of the Angel Street triangle, the rest of the yard already having been turned into lock-up garages.

Peter Upton recalls visiting Grays toward the end of the 1914–1918 war, his father Tom Upton working at that time for King and Chasemore in Horsham. The party set forth for Petworth by train from Horsham to be met at their destination by a privately hired four-wheeler, operated by Henry Streeter, which conveyed them to Angel Street. Henry Streeter would come up from the

Railway Inn to pick them up three or four days later. Grays then had its own turning space in the street opposite so that carriages could sweep round.

Beside Meadow Lodge, another old name for Grays was East Lodge, the name Grays not itself going back much beyond the end of the last century. No one seems to know the origin of the name: an Upton family tradition is that it is a reference to Gray's "Elegy", one of the Upton forbears being particularly interested in poetry, but this seems rather difficult to believe. Upton family documents show that the east wing was added in 1889. This, of course, made the house much bigger than it had been, the new drawing room running right across the house from front to back. The extension cost £1293, a very substantial sum in those days.

The Uptons had lived at Grays for generations until Mitchell Upton sold it in the 1920s. It was said that it had originally been built by the Upton family, and that the stone had come from one of the stone quarries used for rebuilding Petworth House at the turn of the eighteenth century, the incumbent of the great house at the time allowing the Upton family to reopen the quarry just for the stone needed. The stone may in fact have been close at hand; there is a quarry half-way down Shimmings Hill and the almost vertical walls of the Withy Copse seem to indicate a degree of quarrying there at some time.

The Upton family were traditionally professional advisers of various kinds to the big house but many of them seem to have been at the same time in business as entrepreneurs of various kinds, often as estate agents. In latter years the family were well-known for their annual Old Folks Tea in the Iron Room: tea and cakes for the elderly and an entertainment put on by family and friends.

The Withy Copse had been kept up by the family over the years although, by the outbreak of the 1914 war, things were getting much more difficult. Vestiges still remained however of the old tradition of self-sufficiency: there was a cow in the cowshed at the bottom of the steep face of the copse and pasture for her in the meadows. There were chicken too and dovecotes. The path through from Angel Street to Round the Hills was always public but access to the Withy Copse itself was controlled by a gate at the side with latch and bolt. The tennis court was still there when Peter Upton was visiting Grays in the early 1920s and its outline is still clearly visible in the meadow, particularly in a dry season.

Hilldene (Angel Halt) on the north side of the street, and a little way down from the Angel itself, is now a private house with a sizeable walled garden. Traditionally however the premises have been a builders, the builder living in the house and using what is now the garden as a yard. The earliest known photograph of Angel Street shows the old firm of Habbin there. Mr. Habbin was succeeded, it appears, by Mr. Woods and Mr. Woods in his turn by Mr. Cooper a few years before the outbreak of hostilities in 1914. In the 1920s Coopers was still a typical builders and decorators of the time, a self-contained world of paint-kettles, turpentine and distemper brushes. There was a stable in the bottom corner of the yard and like most other builders of the time Coopers still operated with a horse and cart. Quite often, indeed, materials would simply be taken out using the big handcart. These were the days when a painter's toolbag always carried a bottle of "half and half", half linseed oil and half turps to add to the undercoat to thin it down and make application easier. Sid Greest recalled working for Mr. Cooper at Flathurst on the Horsham Road, at that time the Leconfield Estate dairy, and having to use enamel paint for the interior, a somewhat unusual material even then. It was "stiff old stuff" which made the wrists ache. It could not be thinned because the oil would discolour it, all that could be done to make application easier was to leave the can out in the sun for the warmth to thin it a little. In his ten years with Mr. Cooper Sid Greest twice worked on redecorating the Angel, next door but one to Hilldene. "'Morning, Mr. Cooper," I'd say but Mr. Cooper would never return the greeting. "Haven't you got a broom?" he'd reply, "there's stuff blowing all over the street."' Employers were gruff in those days but Coopers were a good firm to work for.

Leconfield Estate contracts were important and they appeared to be shared in such a way that most of the local builders received some work renovating the Estate housing stock. "Cottage-dodging" was the builder's name for this. The old Leconfield colour was stone, a light brown colour and not the present battleship grey. Lord Leconfield was well aware of the proper colour and if a builder miscalculated he might find himself redoing the job. Mr. Cooper was, like many builders of the time, also an undertaker and sometimes Sid Greest would have a day rubbing coffin boards with glass paper to smooth them off. "Every so often the paper would slip and graze my hands so that before long they were running with blood."

Despite Mr. Cooper's strict embargo on smoking in the yard, the men arrived one morning to find the yard burned out. They thought Mr. Cooper would give up, he being at this time by no means a young man, but he rebuilt and carried on. The men were dispatched to work as usual, a very wet, rainy day as Sid Greest recalled.

Angel Street itself has not grown because it backs on to the steep slopes of the Shimmings Valley. Development has been off the road at Sheepdown. From many vantage points the Gog fields can be seen, and, huddled in the valley, the outpost of Shimmings, laid out in the sun or shrouded perhaps in low mist. There is a local tradition that the name Shimmings is derived from the dialect word "shim" meaning a will-o'-the-wisp and referring to Shimmings as sometimes visible and sometimes hidden under a cobweb of mist. The name however seems very old, Leconfield Estate deeds connecting it in late medieval times with the old-established Berkeley family. Shimmings itself is hardly an integral part of Angel Street but the view of it in the distance certainly is. Mount Pleasant up the steps on the south side of the road is aptly named for from here the view of the Gog slopes is magnificent. Valerian grows from the wall here as it does so liberally from the long wall of Grays over the road.

The Roman Catholic Church, noted for its needle spire, is comparatively new. Edwin Saunders writing in the 1960s could remember the building of it as the century turned, although there may be no one left now who can. In his characteristically robust style he relates, "On the road to Pulborough is the Roman Catholic church. I remember it being built very well, a man called Mr. Dawes had it built and . . . stones came from Henley Common near Easebourne and were prepared for building by stone masons. Two houses were built too with pitch pine and varnished over, no paint, one for the priest, the other for nuns".

Mrs. Barnes writing in 1902 is less robust but equally to the point. "Taking the first turn to the left (from East Street) up Angel Street, past the Angel Inn, we come to the Roman Catholic church and house for the priest, built in 1896 by the late Mr. C. W. Dawes of Burton Hill. It is beautifully appointed in every detail. The Angelus is rung daily at 8 am, noon and 6 pm".

On the south side toward the junction with Middle Street is the four-house Montier Terrace, built in 1888 and for long used as police cottages. P.C. Cheney was one of the better known incumbents between the wars. Henry Whitcomb retells the immortal story of the three men who broke Ernest Streeter's Church Street shop window, took some jewellery out of the display cases and made off on foot down North Street. P.C. Cheney set off on his bicycle in pursuit and caught up with them at Limbo. "It's no good you running away," declared the intrepid constable, "you're surrounded." He duly handcuffed the three men to his bike and marched them back to Petworth (*Petworth Society Bulletin* No. 56). Even crime seems to have been rather less sophisticated in those days.

This side of Angel Street was for years the home of the Vincent family, builders and masons. A late Victorian postcard shows a large warehouse-type structure which would later be replaced by the Southdown bus depot. A modern house occupies the position now. The Vincents had a yard to the rear also. At least two classic Walter Kevis pictures show the view of Angel Street looking down toward Middle Street with the celebration bunting out for the Diamond Jubilee of Queen Victoria in 1897 and, five years later, the Coronation of King Edward VII in 1902. The Vincent dog sits quietly beside the road in both pictures as if he had not moved at all through the intervening years. Walking the narrow pavement on the other side of the road one sometimes half expects to see him there still! For such celebrations the Vincents, as many other Petworth residents, made great use of fairy lights — little glass bulbs, somewhat like paste jars but in different colours, which carried squat long-burning candles, strung together to adorn the side of a house.

Ryde House opposite but hidden behind a high hedge is a distinguished house: Stanford Killick a local artist of some note and, apparently, independent means lived there at the close of the nineteenth century. Later it was the home of the Staffurth family, Mr. Staffurth being a prominent local solicitor. The present Portobello, formerly a grain-store belonging to the Milton family, was Olders the grocers, still very well remembered in the town as continuing with the traditional paraphernalia of an old-time grocers into an age which wanted no such things. Here until at least the late 1950s were flour jars, biscuit tins and the smell of coffee beans. The last years were a less glorious compromise with an alien modernity. Like so many such compromises it eventually collapsed. Opposite Olders the bow-window of Polly Whitcomb's shop held a glorious miscellany of cotton-reels, wool and materials. Still recalled by many, it has probably been departed longer than one imagines. These two old-fashioned shops, having survived so long, linger on in the recollection of many but we do not have a full account of them at first hand as we do of many others that succumbed much earlier.

# TREAD LIGHTLY HERE

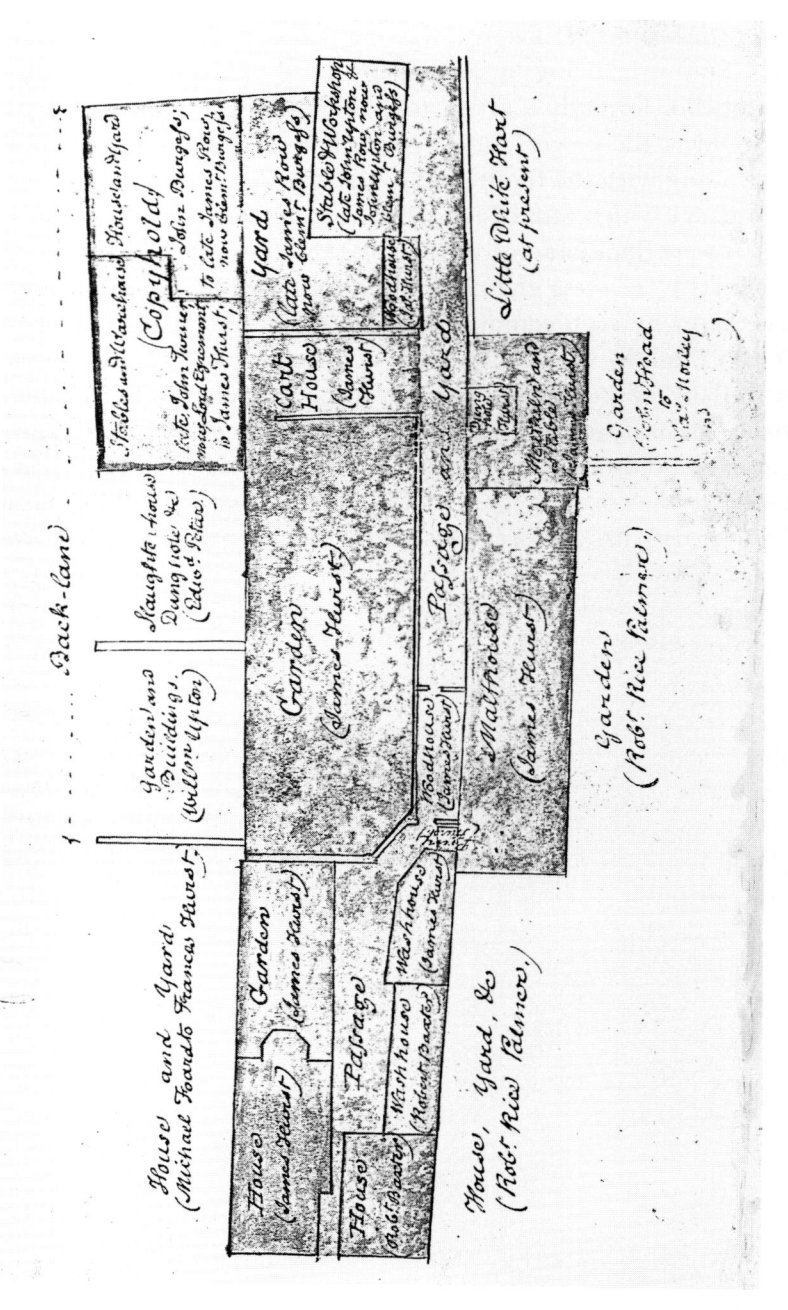

Plan of the land between East Street and Market Square that would be taken for New Street. About 1800. *Petworth House Archives.*

102

# 8

## NEW STREET

THE VERY name New Street strikes an attitude: Petworth after all has had very many additions to its ancient street pattern but New Street is the definitive addition and the name itself gives a certain finality. No other street can be "new" although many have come after. The present New Street effectively closes the canon of Petworth's ancient streets. A sketch map made at the time of the purchase of the land from which the new street would be created shows a narrow passage between the house and garden of James Hurst and the house and washroom of Robert Baxter in Market Square, through James Hurst's woodhouse and out through another passage and yard into East Street (or Back Street as the map confusingly calls it). Basically the new road was driven through gardens and outhouses, removing just the Market Square premises abutting on the present junction, and, as a matter of convenience for traffic, the freestanding Roundabouts House in the Market Square. Master Johnson the tailor would be rehoused nearby. Much of the land and property on which the new road would stand had been tenanted at the turn of the nineteenth century by James Hurst, very probably that same carrier who had once taken John Osborn Greenfield's grandmother to London, in a light cart with one horse, resting the first day at Farnham, at another place the second night and arriving in London about four o'clock on the third day (*Tales* p. 61). The old man had been highly pleased with his progress.

Driven through gardens and outhouses as it was, New Street has ancient property only on its corners. Avenings and Durance at the junction with Market Square, the Red Lion or Little White Hart on one corner of the junction with East Street and in 1800 the premises of Clement Burgess, "architect and stone-mason" on the other. Avenings and Durance are part of the history of Golden Square and Market Square respectively but the Little White Hart, soon to become the Red Lion, is very much integral to New Street. The note on the sketch map "Little White Hart (at present)" may indicate that the change of name was already imminent as the nineteenth century turned; Miss Beck certainly traces the change of name back to roughly this time. The census records from 1841 to 1881 give a different tenant in each decade from George Braby in 1841. Pigot's Directory puts Sarah Watts here in the mid-1820s and makes no bones about referring to the tavern as the Red Lion. In this century the house has been especially associated with the related Purser and Dean families. Jack Purser well remembered the spacious premises being used to billet troops during the 1914-18 war. "They would often drink the place dry and then it would have to close until new supplies came in" (*Petworth Society Bulletin* No. 25). The palliasses used by the troops lingered on in the loft long afterwards. A Walter Kevis photograph, exactly dated in Queen Victoria's Diamond Jubilee year of 1897 shows a somewhat utilitarian brick building with a third storey and a small shop premises in Middle Street; tradition has this as a barber's, while the shop on the west side may have been a tap room.

Over the years the Red Lion, at least as much as any other Petworth hostelry, has been a focal point, a centre for communal consciousness. Without the slightest rational justification I have always connected this particular recollection of Edwin Saunders with the Red Lion as it seems somehow to reflect its spirit. "I knew men who in the spring time of the year would walk to a common so as to hear the nightingale sing, take some strong beer with them and stop for a few hours so as to hear this bird sing. I know my father used to do it. They would get to the common about ten o'clock at night and I have heard them talk about it many times." In less traffic-ridden days the Red Lion corner, as well as the pub itself, was something of a meeting-place. Bill Ede recalled, "Work was never easy to find in those years any more than it is today. Hard weather could put men out and the winter of 1929 was hard. You could see as many as thirty men standing outside the Red Lion in those days; if a man heard of a job he'd tell his friend and so it got around" (*Petworth Society Bulletin* No. 32).

The large shop premises to the west of the Red Lion were for a long while the Hobby Horse tea-rooms but there have been several changes of late years. The International Stores had its premises here

New Street, Mafeking Day 1900. *Photograph by Walter Kevis. Garland Collection.*

from at least 1892 and it seems likely from the census returns that, prior to their coming, the shop had been used as a draper's. G. D. Elmer appears in roughly this position in 1851 and a metal button survives bearing the name "Elmer, Petworth". The indications are that under Henry Kinsey, the next incumbent, the business would eventually move to the bottom of the road but the reasons for this are now quite obscure. The sketch map shows James Hurst's malt kiln and stable as roughly corresponding with the position of the present shop.

The International Stores would move to Otways' old premises in Market Square in the mid-1920s but there is a vivid account by Mrs. Place of the New Street shop well before the 1914-1918 war . . .

> It was a nice friendly shop, lighted like the streets by gas, but the householders had to rely on oil and candles. Very few groceries were packeted so all were weighed. As you entered, on the left was a long wide counter with one or two chairs for the customer's use, with big drawers running under the counter at back containing the goods and some on view on shelves. First were the dried fruits — currants, sultanas, candied peel etc., then the various sugars. A big pair of brass scales in centre of counter and behind the assistant was a glass case showing medical things such as pills, cough cures etc. and on a higher shelf stood big black canisters inscribed in gold paint — CEYLINDO TEA and this was the part allotted to the weighing of it. Price was 4½d. a 1/4 lb. Then at back were rows on rows of big square biscuit tins with the names of contents on them. The favourite ones are much as they are today, but how different the texture. Since the electrical mixers came in the biscuits are so light and thin, one finds many broken ones in the packets, whereas before, they were taken whole from the tins to be weighed, any broken were later put in a tin and children could buy 1 pennyworth of broken biscuits — very popular. After this were the various goods, candles, matches and other household things which were of course packeted.
>
> To separate the counters, was a long iron framed stand, the top shelf showed various nuts, the big Spanish chestnuts at 2d. lb. a great favourite, to roast or boil. The second shelf held apples, lemons and oranges. The latter were the small Spanish variety, which came a little before Christmas, and sold three for 1d. Much

The Red Lion decorated for Queen Victoria's Diamond Jubilee 1897.
*Photograph by Walter Kevis. Garland Collection.*

nicer than the big navel oranges we see now. Lastly, the two lower shelves were for onions, turnips, carrots and potatoes, but I am forgetting, that the end counter before this stand was the one for the various types of flour. When one had completed buying that side it was totted up and you gave the assistant the money which, with the slip stating the amount required he put into a wooden cup, taken from an overhead wire, then it was sent along the wire to the cashiers desk, which stood in a small glass enclosed cabin. The slip was retained and any change was sent back in the same way. You next went over to the right hand for tinned meat such as corned beef, which one could also buy sliced and cooked ham, then the bacon — either joints or rashers cut as preferred, thick or thin. Lastly, on this marble top, were the big slabs of butter and lard to be cut into pieces of required weight, with the wooden butter patts, and patted into shape and wrapped in greaseproof paper. The same process for the payment again. The cashier that I remember was Miss Bessie Rapley and her left arm ended at the elbow, but she managed very well. The manager at that time was Mr. Weaver, who later left and opened his own shop at the lower end of Lombard Street.

I don't think we had all the kinds of biscuits that were in their catalogue, but our favourites were Cracknels made with arrowroot, mostly eaten with a glass of wine, but as children, we liked them with a spoonful of jam, put in the centre, they were boat shaped. Mother liked the Garibaldi, that had plenty of currants in them. The Little Folk and Alphabet letters were liked by little children. Ginger Nuts, never failed, but how I wish we could still find Osborne, Abernethy, and Thick Lunch — a big biscuit to spread with butter, and piece of cheese, they all seemed so much more satisfying. The little ratafia with its almond flavour was used to decorate trifle or Christmas cakes and one I couldn't resist — to my cost. Mother had bought some and put in a tin to use later in that way, and I saw the tin and thought to just try *one*, but that led to many more and when I was discovered as the culprit I had to forgo my Saturday 1d for three weeks.

(Petworth Society Bulletin No. 52.)

Corresponding to the present terrace of houses the sketch map shows a large malthouse belonging to James Hurst and backing onto the extensive garden of Avenings. It was on the site of the malthouse that the new houses would be built. There is little sign of development in the 1841 census, New Street being then much the least populous of all Petworth streets, with William and Charles Johnson, woolstapler and draper respectively, holding sway presumably at the bottom of the street, William Scott maltster and George Braby innkeeper at the top. There would seem to have been a rash of development in the decade after 1841 so much so that New Street would largely assume its present form by 1851. A feature of the census returns from 1851 to 1881 is that these houses have a very low continuity of residence, hardly anyone reappearing from one return to another, quite unlike the other Petworth streets. A little later, but still well before the Great War, Henry Whitcomb recalls the last time that rough music was played in Petworth. It was to censure a man in the terrace who was alleged to have beaten his wife and children. "The crowd carried old tin trays, rattles and drums and would go on for about half an hour before moving off. They might well return however for another burst. The police took no action at all" (*Petworth Society Bulletin* No. 56). Henry Whitcomb's account could come straight out of the pages of *Tales of Old Petworth*.

Whether or not Henry Kinsey the draper had once occupied premises near the Red Lion, there is no doubt that he would eventually have the double-fronted shop at the bottom of the street, its two parts separated by a formidable private-looking house door. One shop is now of course an antique showroom but, for generations, both shops would be connected with the drapery trade, Kinseys, Samuel Dancy, Westlakes and Allans. The census returns from 1851 on suggest that in the mid-century these shops were the premises of Death and Son "auctioneers, valuers, house and estate agents, agents for the sale of foreign wines and spirits, agents for Thorleys cattle food and agents for Lawes' superphosphate and other manures" as Kelly's 1862 directory has it. The next item in the directory gives Death and Son, New Street as "stationer, bookseller, printer and newsagent". It would appear that William Death operated the two shops as separate entities. He was clearly a man of parts and a leading figure in the Petworth of his day.

The Dancy family were popular in early century Petworth and a persistent memory is of being invited to children's parties in the rooms over the shop. Ena Lee vividly recalled one particular game which involved calling the name of one's sweetheart up the chimney, and Mrs. Dancy herself joining in the spirit of the game and shouting her husband's name, "Samuel, Samuel" up the chimney.

Up from the chemists on the northern side of the street the open space now used as car-parking suggests former development on this site, but I think at most there may have been outhouses in this position, backing on to Trump Alley. The 1800 sketch map suggests no more. The story of the northern side of the street is essentially bound up with New Street House and the fortunes of the Knight family, for so long the grocers on the East Street corner.

James Loten Knight, founder of the business, lived in New Street House, the dominating house on this side of New Street. In later years Brenda Knight could well remember her grandfather living there and having one of the upstairs rooms for his tea-blending. He would use the distinctive teamaker's spouted vessel for this. The shop next door was at this time, early this century, an annexe to New Street House and was used as old Mrs. Knight's kitchen. The Knight grandchildren would run through a long passageway in New Street House and turn left at the end into the kitchen. For years Knights smoked their own bacon at the rear of what is now the adjoining shop. Brenda could dimly recall seeing the carcasses hanging on hooks over the fire. Elsie Whitcomb from Pound Street used to speak vividly of how, on May Day, the children would bring their garlands round to the front of New Street House and old Mr. Knight would throw out nuts and oranges for them to "scramble" for. Brenda Knight knew of a similar May Day custom at the cottage in East Street where her parents lived. This time the children were scrambling for bags of sweets. Her mother was always careful to take the house plants out of the window before the celebrations started!

New Street House long survived as a private house although the adjoining premises and the house itself were, after a time, sold by the Knight family. Golds the fishmongers may well have been the first to use the annexe as an out and out shop. The story goes that Mr. Golds the fishmonger had been somewhat off colour and was sent away from Petworth to recuperate. While he was away Mrs.

Golds decided unilaterally to change the shop from a fishmongers to a butchers: she had never liked the smell of fish. When Mr. Golds returned he was a fishmonger no longer. A distinctive fish tile set prominently in the front remained for years as a talking point even when Durrants the butchers were here. It is only of recent years that the tile has been covered but it still remains and perhaps will eventually reappear. It is a genuine piece of "old Petworth".

When New Street House was auctioned in August 1949 the sales particulars described it as "occupying a commanding position in one of the main streets in this old-world town, equally suitable as a Dwelling House or conversion into Business Premises . . ." Prophetic enough: after spells as Petworth Public Library and Petworth Over-60's Day Centre, the big rooms on the ground floor are now the offices of a Building Society. The little shop to the east, used as an Insurance Office, was for years an annexe to the grocers on the corner. It was here that Messrs. Knights kept their crockery and hardware.

Fishmonger turned butcher! This tile on the front of the old butcher's shop tells it all. The tile is still in position but at present covered over.
*Photograph by George Garland. Garland Collection.*

TREAD LIGHTLY HERE

Middle Street June 1950. *Photograph by George Garland. Garland Collection.*

# 9

## MIDDLE STREET

MIDDLE Street, venerable as the name may appear, is in fact one of the newer Petworth street titles. Not that it had, like High Street or Golden Square, an older name, now superseded, simply that in older times it was treated as a mere appendage to East Street. Perhaps "appendage" is a little harsh, it may be more charitable to say that it was the southern end of that long and ancient thoroughfare. The 1882 survey map does not deign to give the street a name at all and the Victorian census enumerators speak only of East Street, using the "Corner House occupied by William Guile" as a dividing line between the district of one enumerator and another. William Guile was a groom and it was of course the position of his house, without a doubt the present Corner Cottage at the junction of Middle Street and High Street that gave him this measure of prominence: his calling, while indispensable, hardly being exalted. Middle Street is not only one of the smallest of Petworth's streets, but is notable too for an unusual imbalance; residential property being concentrated on one side only. This may not always have been so, Treswell's map showing buildings right along the west side in 1610. These may well have been residential at least in part. Unsuitable as it seems for two-way traffic, and slightly removed from the mainstream turning right from East Street into New Street, Middle Street remains a vital link with the southern part of the town.

A familiar Walter Kevis print, perhaps from the late 1870s, shows the corner with Angel Street before the building of the present Card Shop premises. Unfortunately it does not offer a view of Middle Street itself. Mr. Hunt the boot and shoemaker has an appropriately boot-shaped sign hanging up and, in the open doorway, there is a tantalising glimpse of an arm crooked in the characteristic shoemaker's stance. The premises have a delapidated look about them and the east-west alignment is much the same as in

TREAD LIGHTLY HERE

Treswell's map. Had it looked like this in 1610? Fancifully we might think that an ancient hitching-post could once have met Treswell's gaze, but realistically we can have no idea of the changes wrought over such a long period.

The present premises were built for Thomas Leppard the saddler in the 1880s and, by a curious chance, the elevations for the new building have survived in the Leppard family. The indications are that Thomas Leppard was building on an existing business run by the Bryan family. James Edward Bryan, saddler, appears in the 1851 and 1861 census returns, while in 1871 his son Edward Bryan is described as a "master saddler employing one man and one boy". Thomas Leppard would in due course of time give way to A. G. Morley who is half-immortalised in the expression "Morley's Corner" for the junction with Angel Street. I say "half-immortalised" for I fear the expression is falling out of use now. The Morley business flourished over several decades and, when Morley gave up, it devolved on his two employees Fred Sadler and "Nobby" Yallop, the former, appropriately enough, continuing the calling of a saddler and taking the first floor, while Mr. Yallop had the ground floor for bicycles. Mr. Yallop had a large shed to the rear approached from a passageway at the side of Kitts and many an errand-boy will have taken his ill-used trade-bike up to the shed for treatment. In later years Mr. Yallop looked after motor-bicycles too on a small scale.

The formal split in the business, which Mr. Morley had operated as a dual entity for so long, probably indicates the pressures to which the older trade of saddlery was being subjected by the advancing century. The newer venture of bicycles, originally no doubt a sideline, would in later years offer as much or greater potential than the age-old craft of working leather. Gordon Simpson and his sister Sylvia, both now living in Canada, vividly recalled the twilight of the saddlers in the late 1930s and 1940.

"When we were children Grandad was always at work making saddles. He'd be clearly visible at the front upstairs window, sitting on a high stool as he worked at his bench, surrounded by the tools of his trade, awls, leather punches and the rest. He didn't wear old clothes but was always neatly dressed with an apron over his ordinary clothes as he worked . . . What we most remember as children is the unmistakeable clear pungent smell of the new leather".

(*Petworth Society Bulletin* No. 47).

Mr. Morley's emporium in its heyday is recalled in this eulogy from the 1890s.

MR. A. G. MORLEY, SADDLER AND HARNESS MAKER, ATHLETIC OUTFITTER, AGENT FOR CYCLES, PERAMBULATORS, AND SEWING MACHINES, EAST STREET AND ANGEL STREET, PETWORTH.

This important business ranks among the old concerns of Petworth, as it was established more than a century ago, and for that long period has steadily maintained a high reputation. The main line of saddlery and harness is one in which nothing but what is excellent is permissible, and this house has consistently maintained the best traditions of the trade. About five years ago the business was purchased by the present proprietor, who has done much to extend it, both in the leather-working departments and in the others, dealing with cycles, athletic outfits, sewing machines, etc. Mr. Morley has lately been appointed saddler-sergeant of the Middlesex Yeomanry. He is also Hon. Secretary of the Petworth Cycle Club. The premises are at the corner of East Street and Angel Street, and are of three storeys with spacious shop accommodation. One window shows saddlery and leather goods and the other cycles, cricket outfits, etc., the interior being heavily stocked with similar articles such as single, double and draught harness, saddles, portmanteaux, Gladstone bags, whips, horse clothing, brushes, and all kinds of stable requisites, cycles of "crack" make, such as New Rapids and Premiers, for which Mr. Morley is agent, sewing machines by the leading makers, and cycle accessories of all kinds. Mr. Morley is equally noted for carriage harness and draught harness, riding and hunting saddles, all of which he turns out in the best styles, and of the finest materials and workmanship. He enjoys in all departments the patronage of the leading residents and the public generally, and is obviously a popular business man. There is a machinist's department where cleaning, alterations and repairs are carried out promptly at moderate rates.

(*Views and Reviews*)

The two shops that form the present Card Shop premises were at that time separate entities, the more southerly being, for generations, Arnolds the newsagents and stationers. This trade it still follows, although the two Misses Arnold, one tall, lean and angular, the other shorter, are long gone, if still well-remembered by an older Petworth. In the absence of a nineteenth century photograph of Middle Street it is difficult to say what the premises were like prior to Thomas Leppard's rebuilding of the corner site. Arnolds, like most early century stationers, produced picture postcards of local scenes and these are now very much collectors' items.

Kitts (Willow Court) was in the earlier century the home of William Cragg the Bartons Lane plumber, and John Standing, who worked for Craggs in the 1920s, remembers how on Saturday mornings the workmen would troop round to Kitts to collect their wages, Mr. Cragg taking the money off a shelf to pay them. At that time communication with Bartons Lane was via one of the old-fashioned private telephone lines and involved winding a handle, power being provided by a glass "sweet-jar" containing sal-ammoniac. It is likely that a plumbing business had been carried on for some time from these premises, for the 1881 census return gives Mrs. Jane Winter (widow) as carrying on the business of plumber. James Winter her husband had been in charge in 1871. Previous to that the old-established Embling family appear to have lived here. James Embling Junior is described in the 1861 census as a master plumber and glazier employing two men and two boys; his father James Embling is retired and living two doors away. James Embling appears as a plumber and painter in Pigot's Commercial Directory as far back as the mid-1820s. It is possible that Craggs continued this long-existing business: certainly they were notable painters and glaziers. Craggs had their workshop in Bartons Lane but whether their predecessors did is not known.

Kitts is one of Petworth's very ancient house names, going back certainly to Elizabethan times. The origin of the name is not known. Lord Leconfield, writing in *Petworth Parish Magazine* in 1957, gives a tantalising glimpse of its earlier history. The story might, by diligent search at Petworth House, be continued up to James Embling's tenure but equally of course it might not. In any case it would be beyond the scope of this book. Lord Leconfield's note simply gives an idea of what might be available among the Petworth House court books for any ancient Petworth copyhold. The italics are underlined in Lord Leconfield's original . . .

> "Kitts in East Street is first mentioned in January, 1582, when *Robert Braby* was its tenant. In that year he had failed to meet a claim against him for 3s. 10d. due to *Thomas Scott*. The Court therefore ordered *Robert Byrimble,* the Messor, to distrain Robert's goods and thus liquidate the debt. On this order Byrimble entered the premises and seized "a pewter dish, a salver and a woman's gown called a cassock." Three tenants, *John Hatcher, John Kembridge* and *Richard Sutton*, were appointed to value these articles, and they did so at 10s. Thus the debt was amply covered, as was recorded at the court held in May. In 1605 Robert was again in trouble, being accused of extending his boundary, and he was ordered to rectify the trespass under a penalty of 10s. That is the last we hear of him. But he left his mark, and fifty years later Kitts was still described as "late occupied by Robert Brady". It had in fact escheated to the lord of the manor and 1616 had been granted to *William Bowyer*. It remained his until 1653 when he sold it to *Robert Trewe* the plasterer. In his hands it remained until he died in 1682. By his will it passed to his son Robert for life, with remainder to his grandson Robert."

An escheat is a reversion to the Lord of the Manor, owing usually to an absence of legal heirs. Wills and inventories survive for the Trew family but there are two distinct Petworth branches and it is not always easy to distinguish members of one branch from members of another. In the 1920s motorised traffic in Middle Street was still sufficient of a novelty to permit a sandwichboard to stand out in the street extolling the virtues and carrying a portrait of the Liberal candidate at a forthcoming General Election.

Keytes is the next house along the row and the similarity in name with neighbouring Kitts has often been a source of confusion. There can be no such confusion with the next house "Alfreston House", not I would think an old name. For many decades this was the home of the Downs family, latterly of the two sisters Mabel and Katie. There was a sitting-room on the left while the room on the right was used as a coal-office. Coal could be ordered here and accounts paid. Mabel looked after the office while her sister Katie managed the house and garden. Both sisters were somewhat hard of hearing and the Sunday morning hymns on the wireless would sound out into Middle Street while the dog sought refuge in the long garden! The long strips of garden are a feature of these houses.

The two houses to the south of the Downs' were basically cottages: the more northerly having a sitting-room, kitchen and scullery on the ground floor. Mr. Boxall, who worked for the Leconfield Estate, went there in 1914 and would remain for several decades. There was a gigantic hook in the kitchen which "would have held a bullock" and it was never considered safe to interfere with this somewhat disconcerting heirloom in case it undermined the whole structure. No doubt it has gone now but it certainly made papering the ceiling a complex and awkward procedure. Tradition had it that the premises had once been a butcher's but this may simply have been a deduction from the presence of the giant hook. Certainly the census returns, as far as they go, do not seem to substantiate this tradition although one certainly has to say that eighteenth and early nineteenth century Middle Street is at present something of a lost world.

Mr. and Mrs. Curtis lived in the adjoining cottage between the wars and Mrs. Curtis for a long time after, her husband having worked at different times for the Leconfield Estate and Boxalls the Tillington builders. Next door in the house on the corner, once William Guile's, lived Mrs. Maybank, widow of the East Street coachbuilder, and later of course Bert Speed, the High Street butcher. Well before the Maybanks came, Mrs. Boxall along the road was on her own when a thunderstorm came up. Her daughter had just been born and the new mother was terrified of thunderstorms. Going to the back door in search of succour of some kind, she looked right across the neighbouring strip of garden to the back door of the Corner House. Her elderly neighbour was standing at the back door too and called across, albeit kindly, "I would have you in here dear, but you haven't been churched yet". In its own way a charitable remark, in no way bigoted, it yet reflects perhaps as much as anything in this book a century of changing attitudes and torpedoed certainties.

The shop at the west corner of Middle Street (now Petworth Provisions) has been a bakery for most of this century — first Todmans, then, after 1915, Hazelmans. In the early days bread was delivered by horse and cart and the ponies were kept in the old stable yard just along the road where the vans would later be garaged. This has now been converted to shop premises.

In early days Percy Hazelman had as regular staff only his wife and a boy with a hand-cart. The shop, as well as being a baker's, sold general provisions and butter, lard and bacon; all had to be laboriously measured out and packed from bulk. Salt blocks had to be sawn. He would be in the bakehouse by five o'clock each morning, hand-making the dough and getting the wood and coal-fired oven ready for baking. Christmas was the busiest period, Percy Hazelman recalling that he once baked five thousand loaves with only a little help from a man coming in at 1 am to "scale off" the dough (*Petworth Society Bulletin* No. 23).

Days in the bakehouse between the wars are vividly remembered by Bill "Duckie" Herrington in *Petworth Society Bulletin* No. 36 . . .

"Two of us worked in the bakehouse and we kept the flour in the loft above. When we needed a bag we would hand it down to the man in the bakehouse below. Each sack weighed a hundred-weight and a quarter and it was a job to do in the morning when we wouldn't be under quite so much pressure. Dough-making would begin about six in the evening. We'd have two great bins and put two and a half hundred-weight of flour in each, inserting a pen-board to keep the flour and the water separate. You'd weigh up six pounds of salt and put it in with six buckets of water adding liquid malt to keep the bread moist and a pound of yeast or, if the weather was cold, a pound and a quarter and mixing it in with the liquor. You'd then knead, shaking out the scraps i.e. the odd lumps of flour and water and putting them back into the other side of the bin, then as you worked up toward the end of the bin, cut the dough with your knife, punch it and work it and force it to the other side of the bin, all the time scraping the bin's sides so that nothing was wasted. Then you'd cut the dough again, punching it down to the bottom of the bin. When you had kneaded the contents of the bin thoroughly you would put sacks over the top to keep it warm and let it lie there until four in the morning. First thing in the morning you would "scale" it, dividing the dough into pieces of roughly 2lbs 3ozs to allow three ounces of weight loss in the baking, then moulding or "harding" them up to the required shapes before proving. White loaves might be long tins, square tins, sandwich, cottage, coburg or the long "french" loaves. They would be set to prove and we'd then turn our attention to the brown bread — Hovis, Turog, Wholemeal — there were eight or nine different sorts. When the dough was ready we'd fill the oven, still faggot-fired in those days. Each oven took over a hundred loaves and while they were baking we'd get ourselves up for the next lot. We'd go on till all the dough was used — perhaps two in the afternoon. It would then be time to smarten up, load up the pony cart and set off.

Mr. Hazelman kept chicken in his back yard and I remember the rooster running into the bakehouse and without thinking scuttling straight into the oven. We got him out but the experience had taken all his feathers off. We let him loose in the yard and eventually his feathers started to grow again. Mr. Jones at the workhouse wanted a cockerel to go with his hens and asked Mr. Hazelman if he had one: "There's one here with no feathers," he was told, "but they're coming." He took it and reckoned in the end it was the best rooster he'd ever had."

Middle Street is dominated, effectively hemmed in, by the Club Room that stands opposite the junction with High Street. Although a part of High Street, the Club Room is most obvious as one looks down the short length of Middle Street. In days when traffic was less frequent and frenetic than it is now, the Middle Street children would stand out in the roadway and look up at the apex of the Club Room roof where reigned a gleaming weather vane, shaped like a fish and made of copper or brass. As it whirled round with the breeze the rays of the sun cascaded from the golden fish. One wind-swept night the marvellous weather vane came clattering down, never to be restored to its old glory, never, rumour has it, ever to be seen again. The Club Room was home to the Girl Guides under Miss Upton and Miss Staffurth, as of course it was home to so much else. Mr. Spurgeon, the High Street vet, and Mrs. Spurgeon would ride out to hounds, coming through Middle Street in their hard hats. Once Mr. Spurgeon came riding through Middle Street with his hard hat surmounted by the tammy his wife so often wore. Mrs. Boxall in Middle Street didn't like to approach him: it was not her place she thought so she let him go on with his curious headgear intact. Such were the attitudes in those days. Those who rode to hounds were, to an extent, a race apart.

Middle Street about 1920. An Arnold postcard. *Mr. G. Botwright, Newhaven.*

TREAD LIGHTLY HERE

Grove Street about 1899. *Photograph by Walter Kevis. Garland Collection.*

## 10

## GROVE STREET

GROVE Street, extending from the junction of High Street with Rosemary Lane in the direction of Haslingbourne is a comparative newcomer among Petworth's ancient streets, not quite the parvenu that is New Street, but a newcomer nevertheless. Certainly, like Station Road it is an ancient thoroughfare, but a glance at Treswell's map shows hardly a house along the road. Soanes, of course, away at the end of the lane is old and Arnold's *History* (p. 88) knows of a family called de Aula or Atte Hall established in the region of New Grove in the early fifteenth century but there is little or nothing else in the way of settlement that is demonstrably ancient. Something of an exception may be the three cottages next up from New Grove towards Petworth, traditionally known as the World's End and in later years simply as World's End. The property is described in PHA deeds OG 17/5 as a freehold messuage and tenements with garden and premises in the possession of Thomas Pearson and James Hopkins and bounded on the north-east by the road or street leading from Petworth to Sutton and on the south by New Grove garden "scituate or being at a place called the World's End". One house seems older than the others for there is mention in 1791 of "all the three messuages, tenements or dwelling-houses (two of which were lately erected or then in erecting)". The original premises had been sold by the Earl of Egremont to Thomas Pearson who is described in a burial certificate of July 1814 as "porter to the Earl of Egremont". The complex mortgage history of the property would later be tidied up with its repurchase by Colonel Wyndham in 1841. The census returns to 1851 do not in fact speak of Grove Street at all, the name appearing in its own right only in 1861. World's End appears at this time to be a general name for the whole street, gradually demoted in successive returns to cover a smaller and smaller area until it simply reverts virtually to its old use for the three cottages in the shadow of the New Grove rookery. The usage

World's End seems now to have passed out of use altogether, a victim perhaps of its own lack of pretension. Back Street, the Beast Market and the Causey have suffered a similar fate and we may well regret their passing.

In days before the main road was brought over Shimmings and the road from Horsham did not come further than Fox Hill, World's End provided one of the four main entrances into Petworth, even if not, perhaps, the most frequented. A minute in the Churchwarden's Vestry Book for 24th December 1811 lays down that all vagrants found within the parish limits are to be taken before a Justice of the Peace for the purpose of being committed to prison and that anyone who discovers such a vagrant be requested to inform the constable or tithingman. Notices to this intent were to be placed at the bottom of Pound Street and North Street, at or near the Angel and "at or near New Grove". A very early photograph taken, it would seem, roughly where the present private road leads away to Cherry Orchard, shows Grove Street much as it is today. The houses on the left hand looking up toward High Street are traditionally Warders' cottages and may well have been built around the turn of the nineteenth century. The great gaunt structure of the prison dominates the street as it would do for most of the nineteenth century.

"Eight minutes from Square", as Mrs. Barnes tersely reminds us (*Petworth* p. 16) is New Grove, temporary domicile of Grinling Gibbons while he worked on the carvings in Petworth House. The present imposing residence may not be the only house erected on this site; an early seventeenth century transfer speaks already of a "superior house lately built" (Leconfield, *Petworth Manor* p. 124). The freehold appears to have passed at about this time from William Goble to John Hall, and in the course of time to John Hall's daughter who married first William Peachey and then Henry Bulstrode. It is to Bulstrode that Arnold attributes the building of the present house (*History* p. 89). Long the home of the Peachey family it was eventually sold to the Earl of Egremont in 1773. In latter years it was the residence of the Agents to the Leconfield Estate and for a period the home of the author A. E. W. Mason.

An interesting sidelight on nineteenth century New Grove comes from a file of correspondence between the tenant at that time and Lord Leconfield concerning his desire for her to vacate the premises to accommodate Mr. Ingram, his new agent (PHA 734). The tenant is Mrs. Edith Robinson, widow of John Henry Robinson (1796-1871) the engraver, and the tone of the corresponding gives the impression of a decidedly strong-willed lady. Having been told on her husband's death that her tenure was secure, she now, some two years later, finds herself asked to move to other accommodation. "I could hardly believe it," she writes, "for I thought as you said I was to remain at New Grove it was quite equal to a lease". Mrs. Robinson looks back to New Grove when the two of them had come there first in the early 1850s. The garden had nothing but laurels and hollies and "all the paths even the foundation of them" had to be put in. The kitchen garden was devoid of fruit trees except for some very old apple trees and an old apricot tree. All the present trees had been planted by herself and Mr. Robinson and she does not wish to leave them. In addition her furniture will not fit into a smaller house: it had cost £300 to bring it from London.

Lord Leconfield's replies suggest a certain unease coupled with a determination to hold firm. He probably felt his initial undertaking to Mrs. Robinson had been a little rash, occasioned perhaps by sympathy at her husband's death as much as by prudence. The correspondence takes on a more acerbic tone when Mrs. Robinson demands very substantial improvements to a proposed alternative house at Tillington. A final offer from Lord Leconfield is dated 23rd May 1873 and gives a definite impression of fraying patience, and it is probable that Edith Robinson had to make the best of what was, from her point of view, a thoroughly bad job. She certainly gives the impression of a lady who is well able to fight her own corner.

John Henry Robinson had been elected R.A. in 1867 and the R.A. Summer Exhibition lists show four engravings exhibited between 1854 and 1864. He appears to have specialised in engraving portraits and, in his earlier career, in engraving for book illustration. Benezit in his Dictionary of Artists notes that he was a pupil of James Heath and adds, "Un marriage advantageux lui permit de se retirer en province où il mourut". Edith Robinson appears to have been a wealthy woman.

The dominance of the great house and its effect on the rest of the street is well captured by Henry Whitcomb in this recollection of the early century (*Petworth Society Bulletin* No. 33). The Whitcomb family lived in what is now Regency Cottage, a little up the road and on the opposite side from "the Grove".

> "We used to keep pigs when we lived in Grove Street and would take on any empty sty that was going on the nearby allotments. On Sundays I had to be careful with my bucket of pig swill for Mr. Watson, the agent, lived at New Grove and when the family drove to church in their carriage and pair I was not to be seen carting pig swill about. "Hang on," my father would say, "they haven't gone along yet". We'd kill two pigs a year and salt them down ourselves in the cellar of the house in Grove Street, once the old Fox and Hounds pub. Salting was my job, using the big old yellow sinks in the pub cellar. There I would rub in the salt and brown sugar, and as the juices ran out, ladle the brine over the bacon and turn it. This I had to do every day."

There is certainly a reference to the Fox and Hounds in the 1861 census but it may well have been one of those short-lived beerhouses that are so difficult to trace. Henry Whitcomb continues . . .

> My father and grandfather were builders and there weren't too many builders in Petworth in those days. Much of our work was for Leconfield but we did private work too. Much of our Estate work was on farms and some were so outlying that we would go away for the week. Applesham Farm at Shoreham was one of these. My father would leave Grove Street in the early hours of Monday morning, six men altogether in a horse and cart, work all week, and then set off back on Saturday half-day (four o'clock). They'd get back about ten in the evening ready to start off again on Monday.

The story of the Grove Street houses on the north side as far as Percy Row is not easy to tell. In a way Henry Whitcomb's account of his father's somewhat itinerant building business illustrates this: the pattern appears to be one of artisans basically working away from the street. The census records offer little that strikes a chord, there is a blacksmith and a whitesmith, and in fact indications of iron-working of some kind have been found on the corner by the private road to Cherry Orchard, the road itself being a relative

GROVE STREET

"New Grove for Mr. Ingram." No date but probably about 1885.
*Photograph by Walter Kevis. Garland Collection.*

innovation. A Smithy is shown here on the 1874 OS map. A turn of the century photograph is captioned "Mr. McLachlan's house," but Mr. McLachlan would later live elsewhere in Petworth. Muskett Cottage is a modern name, a conscious recollection of Mr. Musket who so assiduously cultivated his allotment for so long. The apple tree and the shed on the far side of the road to Cherry Orchard were once part of his domain. Percy Row too has left little obvious mark on history. Nairn (pp. 198-9) describes it as "a long terrace with heavy chimneys, segment-headed windows, coupled barge-boarded porches. The details are almost those of the 1720s." In fact Percy Row appears to be mid-Victorian with the generous cottage gardens that the Leconfield Estate provided for its workers in those days. Tradition has it that every house had its cherry tree. There would no doubt have been much clanging of bells as artful birds sought to pre-empt the fruiting season.

What would have dominated nineteenth century Grove Street is the austere towering pile of the prison, rising Leviathan-like on the south side of the road and dwarfing the warders' cottages that line the road. Built in 1788 and designed by James Wyatt, Petworth gaol replaced the desperate old Bridewell visited by Howard the philanthropist in 1774 and 1776 and usually located roughly in the same Fairfield area. It was in part the very inhumanity of the old Bridewell that led gradually to reform. Arnold's *History* gives some harrowing details from Howard's journal and observes, "It was customary for the inmates to put out a leather bag with a label on it, 'Pray remember the poor prisoners'." (p. 94.) The old Bridewell, said the magistrates appointed to look into the situation, was "in every respect improper for the purpose intended, no conceivable alteration would render the place fit."

Suggestions for a new prison were not well received locally and a petition survives in the Quarter Sessions Records at the West Sussex Record Office claiming that the plan was too expensive and seeking an outlay of not more than £1,000. The protest was to no avail and the Fairfield site was put at the County's disposal by the Earl of Egremont. Dallaway's History gives some details: the prison was of two storeys over arcades, each room containing an iron bedstead, straw mattress and bolster, two blankets and a quilt. There were infirmaries on each floor and a chapel in the centre with thirty-two high sided pews. The high sides would prevent prisoners communicating. In 1816 the principle of solitary confinement was ordered to be implemented and the arcades were filled up on the ground floor, effectively creating another storey. A woollen manufactory was established to make cloth. By 1820 a treadwheel had been installed for those sentenced to hard labour and a printed directive of 1823 survives covering its use. Twelve prisoners were to be worked on the wheel, nine on the wheel at a time with three as relief. The three relief would be replaced every fifteen minutes.

A new governor, John Mance, was appointed in 1826 and under him an already austere regime seems to have become more so. In September 1831 he informs Mr. Langridge, Clerk of the Peace at Lewes, that the diet of the prison is "seven ounces of the best wheaten flour boiled in water to make a quart of thick gruel or rather hasty pudding and seasoned with salt for breakfast, and one and a half pounds of the best wheaten bread daily". Langridge is clearly querying the austerity of the regime at Petworth but Mance stands his ground: "I have now," he goes on, "a notorious vagrant in my custody who declared to me, in the presence of the prisoners working on the treadwheel, that he would rather be three months in Lewes Prison than one in this House and he assures me to his great satisfaction that he will never come into this division of the county again". Mance was something of a pioneer in his field and increased the provision for hard labour at Petworth by constructing a graduating pump to operate in conjunction with the treadwheel. Petworth could impose hard labour on thirty prisoners at a time. He also invented an instrument called an Ergometer which measured the daily amount of labour exerted on the treadwheel over a period of three months. The soul-sapping character of all this was that it produced no useful work. It was simply punishment or "correction" for its own sake. Petworth Gaol was indeed a "house of correction".

The solitary confinement system began to break down in the face of an increasing prison population in the early 1830s and further structural alterations were made in 1834. In 1843 Horsham prison closed and arrangements had to be made for Petworth to become "a new common gaol as well as a house of correction" i.e. to take a number of special prisoners such as debtors. Mance left in 1856 to be replaced by William Linton and the new governor is soon writing of "alteration in the discipline and arrangements". John Mance had indeed been a model of austerity. Under Linton the prison regime, while harsh indeed by modern standards, seems to have left at least some of the excesses of the old regime behind. Numbers gradually dwindled after 1856. Perhaps the most significant comment on changing times comes in this casual observation by the chaplain Alexander Combes in October 1869, "In this period there has been the usual influx of travelling thieves and disorderly persons who are drawn to the towns upon our sea-coast by the attractions offered in the summer months". The prison was demolished about 1880 and the police force, for which Petworth was at this time the County Headquarters, took over the governor's house and two other houses. West Sussex Police HQ remained at Petworth until 1897 when it was moved to Horsham. There is a fuller account of Petworth Gaol in *Petworth Society Magazine* Nos. 30, 31, and 32 and a first-hand account of working at the Gaol in the late 1870s in Nos. 49 and 50.

Away off the road in the area of the present Courtlea and Lund House was the Red House, home of Colonel and Mrs. Simpson. Edith Sumersell recalled its early century heyday as a large house . . .

"Back once more at Petworth I began work as housemaid for Colonel and Mrs. Simpson at the Red House off Grove Street. As house parlour-maid I used to get up at about 6.30 in the morning and go round doing the dining room and drawing room grates before cleaning the scullery and kitchen, I'd then lay the table for breakfast. Ethel Puttick the cook, and I had our meals together in the kitchen. Part of the cook's job was to black lead the stove. I remember the house as having very high ceilings and fairly extensive outbuildings. I'd begin upstairs and work my way downstairs: cleaning was all dustpan and brush work in those days. The washing was put out to local people to be done as was the custom then in most large houses. Mrs. Simpson lived on at Red House for quite a long time after she was widowed, I remember her coming to church for my wedding although I had left her employ by then. The Simpsons were nice people I always thought. Life was very ordered in such a household: visitors would come for tea, the vicar perhaps or one of the doctors. Occasionally one of the family would come down to stay for a few days. Mrs. Simpson insisted that we went to church on Sundays."

*(Petworth Society Magazine* No. 55)

The 1874 Ordnance Survey map clearly delineates the extensive prison complex and a photograph shows the high wall still in place in 1920 before the present Magistrates' Court was built. The Magistrates' car park wall has obviously used bricks from the old prison. Dates and names from the early nineteenth century can still be easily made out incised in the brickwork. The photograph shows too the Royal British Legion hut, partly built on what in 1874 was described as a covered reservoir. The RBL was known in those days as the Comrades of the Great War and church parades would traditionally start from here in Grove Street. Grove Street in fact was the starting point for most Petworth processions, the Scouts in early days falling in at New Grove, their HQ, and marching to church for eleven o'clock service, drum and bugle band and Scout standard to the front, Cubs to the rear.

The spirit of Grove Street is difficult to pin down but a spirit of its own it undoubtedly has. There are no shops, and development has been later and more sporadic than in other Petworth streets. The extensive grounds of New Grove have always given its further reaches a certain leafy, almost suburban, quiet. Not even the hurricane of 1987 has entirely dispelled this. There is a quiet as one walks the pavement beside the New Grove wall that no other Petworth street can command. Perhaps it is that Grove Street has been the last Petworth street to lose its age-old links with agriculture. Vernon Hawkins recalled the days a half-century or more ago when the Grove Lane council houses were new built and the garden fence was a frontier on another world. Once over the fence and into Soanes he could help Mr. Townsend the shepherd feed the sheep or put them out on the turnips. Mr. Townsend had a curious kind of hoe which he used to prise the roots out of the ground when the sheep had nibbled away the top part. Quarry Farm was away up the lane on the other side of the road and the barn, now a private house, would often have a horse "podging" round, turning a chaff-cutter.

TREAD LIGHTLY HERE

Converted house premises in High Street October 1945. *Photograph by George Garland. Garland Collection.*

# 11

## HIGH STREET

PARADOXICALLY for a high street, at least to our twentieth century eyes, Petworth's version lies off the main vehicle routes through the town. This lack of through traffic does not in fact give any great relief, for on-street parking on the north side diminishes the view, gives a cramped feeling and effectively reduces traffic to a single line. A measure of dexterity is needed to park in High Street at all! Busy without being bustling, High Street is clearly an old foundation, but it has stood over the centuries on the very edge of historic Petworth and just a hint of this independent character still remains. Its history is perhaps as difficult to unravel as that of any other single Petworth street: a certain distance from the great house making in its turn for a certain dearth of record. High Street itself is a relatively modern name: the 1882 Estate survey map talking of "High Street or Back Street" as if the two were synonymous in current usage. "Back Street" would seem the more venerable title while "High Street" would be championed by the resident shopkeepers as being the more prestigious. When New Street was created at the beginning of the nineteenth century, diverting as it did such through traffic as there was at that time, the street would have felt very much out of the way of things — something of a backwater perhaps and Back Street an apt enough name.

As if to compound possible confusion, the 1882 survey map adds, "also called East Street or South Street or Red Lion Street". No other Petworth street has had such a crisis of identity over the years. East Street seems almost slighting, as if to say that the street should be considered no more than an appendage to East Street and its continuation Middle Street. The connotation of South Street is obvious but again suggests it is merely part of East Street, East Street sometimes being known as South Street. Red Lion Street is probably as old and distinctive a name as any, referring as it does to an ancient inn to the south of the later Queen's Head, and clearly marked in italic lettering on the 1882 survey. Treswell's map shows High Street already as well-defined in 1610 with houses on either side of the road but becoming noticeably sparser after the junction with Middle Street. John Ederton's rent return does not obviously refer to properties in this street but the Manorial Court (11th September 1666) castigates one Francis Eaton "for laying his dounge and earth in the South Street and doe amerce him therefor iid and that he remove the same by the twentieth of this month upon paine of five shillings" (PHA 3955). We have once more the ambiguity that the reference may be to the present East Street or even Middle Street!

Within living memory the north side of the street has been a mix of commercial and domestic premises, shop and living accommodation often going together in earlier years. Of later years the preponderance has been commercial. Bromhams at the bottom were remote forerunners of Petworth's more recent explosion of antique shops. An entry in Kelly's 1918 Directory gives Mrs. Violet Bromham as an antique dealer: she is remembered as specialising particularly in period furniture. Kelly's gives the address as Golden Square but in fact the shop is remembered as being on the north side of High Street and facing across the road. Bromhams are now at the very limit of recollection, the business not surviving much beyond the end of the war. For a period the shop window was used as a plumber's showroom displaying a somewhat sparse assortment of sanitary ware and similar requisites.

The gap to the east, still existing, led to garages at the rear used by "Pym" Purser for her taxi service, and a house since demolished. On the other side of the gap four steps led up to a fish and chip shop with living accommodation. The steps are clearly visible in such early century photographs of High Street as exist. Alterations by Charles Leazell the builder here, as elsewhere in High Street in the late 1920s, produced a larger shop premises, initially the Blue Bowl tea-room, run by Mr. Arnold, at one time chauffeur at New Grove, and his wife. The shop would soon become the Petworth headquarters of the Southern Electricity Board.

Phyllis Catt vividly recalls a brief stay here in the late 1920s. (*Petworth Society Bulletin* No. 58.)

"The house in High Street was, I thought, very disappointing. It was in a row with no garden, just a little yard at the back where we put a few hens. There was a space for the car at one side, no electricity, but that was nothing new to us.

The previous tenant had turned the large front lounge into a Tea-room. My mother disliked the huge shop windows so she locked up the front door in the centre which opened on to the pavement, and hung muslin curtains the complete height. We could then see out, but no one could see into the room. The main entry was made from the 'Car-Port' as it would be called today, into a small office. The front room was very large with an ingle nook fireplace. Upstairs there were two double bedrooms in front and a smaller bedroom and a bathroom at the back.

At the further end of the passage were two very high wooden doors kept locked, and inside was the garage for Pym Purser's two hire cars. We used to hear the men working in there. If the weather was very hot they would throw open the big doors to let some air through. In February 1929 we had an extremely cold spell with no water in the mains of High Street. A cart brought water round for two weeks, and all the horses had their shoes roughed for the icy roads."

Next up was Mr. Herbert the shoe-repairer, who had a small premises at the front, "a mere sliver of a shop" and a large room at the back where he worked at his shoe-repairing. The front shop was used for greengrocery and Mr. Herbert would appear from his workshop when the bell sounded. As so often, the bulk of the frontage was taken up by a living room at the side. The present shop is another Leazell conversion, incorporating the large room at the side into the shop premises. It would become Peacocks, then Lerwills, the butchers, then of course Speeds. Ironically the premises immediately adjoining, for generations Deans the fishmongers, had been in the early century a butchers: Knight and Co. Melicent Knight looking back to the outbreak of the 1914-1918 war and earlier gives us the most detailed account of a High Street shop that survives.

"I was born in High Street where Deans the fishmongers later had their shop. Like so many of Petworth's old shops, the premises now house antiques. The shop is still recognisably the same, even to the red and blue tiling on the floor. The shop had formerly been Knights the butchers and my father took over as proprietor about 1906. One of my earliest memories is of watching the pigs being "stuck" in the alleyway opposite. The pig's throat would be cut and the blood carefully collected in a vessel. Petworth House would take the blood to make black puddings, a great delicacy then. I suppose that watching such scenes as a child was in a real sense more violent than today's television or video but as I had been born into it I am not aware of it upsetting me, it was simply a part of everyday life. Our slaughter-house was at the bottom of the Alley: all the Petworth butchers had their own separate slaughter-house at this time. The animals would be brought in by the farmers in carts and would usually be docile enough until they caught the smell of the slaughter-house, the whiff of blood hanging on the air. Then they could be very difficult. Animals were still "poleaxed" with a blow on the head at this time before the humane killer and the carcasses had to be dragged out of the alley across High Street and into the shop. Dad would look out of the alley to see if there were any strong men coming up the road who would help to drag the carcass into the shop for it to be skinned and cut up.

Butchers bought their meat on the hoof then. On Sundays if the weather was fine the whole family would go around the neighbouring farms like Frog or Stag Park and discuss forthcoming purchases with the individual farmers. The other Petworth butchers did the same. When cut up the meat would be left to hang for a while in the big store at the back of the shop. There was of course no refrigeration but there was already a twice-weekly delivery of ice. This came from Guildford by lorry and was particularly welcome in summer. The ice came in enormous blocks and was picked up by huge metal tongs. The blocks were laid on sacks and manhandled into the shop. We kept them as best we could but, big blocks as they were, the ice was a fragile thing and tended to disappear all too quickly from the baths and tubs in which we tried to keep it. For us children it was a great treat to sneak into the store and take piece of ice to chew. Not very hygienic I suppose by today's standards."

(*Petworth Society Bulletin* No. 51.)

Mr. Dean the fishmonger was a real character with an uncanny ability to throw his voice and quite capable not only of threatening a cheeky boy with a policeman but also of making the policeman's

HIGH STREET

Mr. Dean the fishmonger. High Street 1920s. *Mr. E. Delderfield, Tillington.*

gruff voice issue from the back of the premises. He might even get a fish to talk to an unsuspecting bystander — from the slab! Mr. Lugg the farmer from Gunter's Bridge would always greet him with, "Good morning, your honour, Mr. Dean".

The next shop up is yet another Leazell conversion, now Corralls. Here a private house has been turned into a shop. Mr. Jerry the tailor was here in the 1930s, while a Garland photograph from 1946 shows the British Field Sports Society with an office there. The passageway at the side led to three cottages at the rear occupied in the 1920s by Mrs. Moore, Mrs. Tiplady and Mrs. Saunders. Mrs. Saunders worked in the bothy in Lord Leconfield's gardens looking after the young gardeners who lived in. Across the passage was Whethams the grocers, and from a little annexe to Whethams Mr. Gallup operated his clothing business, travelling round with his wares. Hazelmans, formerly Todmans, were on the corner. Whethams, so long a grocers, had in the early century been two shops, Mrs. Tiplady's sweet shop occupying one part of the premises and Walter Stedman having the other part for pots, pans and crockery. He is listed in Kelly's 1918 Directory as an ironmonger. When Mr. Smith came out of the Army after the Great War he converted the two shops into a single general store and lived on the premises. He bought one of the very early motor cars for deliveries and had A. C. Smith embossed in large porcelain letters on the windscreen. Carrying on to an extent the Stedman business, he sold clothes, boots and shoes, chicken feed, paraffin, fruit and vegetables. Even at this time Mr. Gallup is remembered as setting off on foot on his rounds, walking right out into the country in his bowler hat and carrying his stout stick with the parcels tied to it.

Over the road Harry Greest the blacksmith had his forge, once Southins, continuing in business until the late 1940s in face of a declining demand for his services in latter years. Arthur Stevens the shoe repairer would work from these premises after him but by the late 1960s they were in some disrepair. A famous Garland picture shows Harry Greest shoeing on the other side of the road against the White Hart in 1939. Photographers often look for the unusual rather than the everyday and thus it is by this dramatic but untypical picture that the forge is now recalled. On that day an unusually large waggon had taken possession of the forge while Jack

Miles the carter from Coxland, Tillington had been fencing and cut his hand badly. He was on light duties and light duties did not preclude his bringing Punch down to the smith's to be reshod. Just further up was Ricketts' yard. They were coal merchants and station carriers, and, in the days before the internal combustion engine, an essential element in any school outing, private picnic or festive occasion. Later the yard would be Whitingtons' the plumbers.

On the other side of the road is Stone House, sometime used as a manse for the Congregational minister, although the house to the rear, through what Nairn describes as "an elegant and reticent iron arch", has also fulfilled that function and still bears the name. Nairn enthused about this corner of Petworth and approved the "perfect little C18 front" of Stone House. Its history is not well-documented but it will at least have been the home of a wealthy tradesman. Mrs. Watson had the house for a period in the 1950s, letting rooms as she had in those now far-off days when young curates began their careers as assistants at Petworth. She is better remembered in Park Road. Stone House at that time belonged to the Leconfield Estate.

On the lower floor of what is now Stoneycroft was Harry Seldon's hairdressing, not so much a shop as a living-room made over. Country hairdressers usually operated like this between the wars. The long gardens to the west were once built on, the houses probably abutting on to the High Street, although no photograph of them survives. Mrs. Gumbrell recalls: "I was born in Petworth in 1891 but we left for Byworth when I was a baby. My parents were the last tenants in a cottage in High Street that was pulled down about this time. There are now gardens on the site . . . I don't remember the old cottages that were there and their replacements were built to the back" (*Petworth Society Bulletin* No. 48).

The present houses to the west side are built on the site of the old High Street corn windmill, described in a sale poster from 1848 as "with five floors, carrying two pairs of stones, and proper machinery". The front of the property "abutting to the Back Street" was some 45 feet wide to about 89 in depth, "after which it widens to about 79 feet by a further depth of 113 feet making the whole depth 202 feet, affording ample space for any business". In due course the windmill would be pulled down to make way for a new Infants' School, in its turn to be replaced by the Public Library.

Windmill House across the lane is a conversion from an original pair of cottages, George Garland the photographer purchasing them from the Leconfield Estate in the mid-1950s and moving up into the town from Station Road. As a boy he could remember an old lady selling seeds in the left hand cottage but never dreamed that one day he would actually live there. The name Windmill House is George Garland's own conscious recollection of the windmill. It was an irony that he who had taken so many pictures over the years should be unable to find what he would so much have liked: a picture of the old windmill! A sales poster of 1848 was the nearest he would come but sales posters in 1848 did not carry illustrations. The poster mentions also a wheelwright's shop and this would have been a long-established business by 1848: in the late eighteenth century John Greenfield from Byworth rented the annexe to Windmill House as a wheelwright's and sub-let the adjoining premises to tenants. In 1786 he bought the shop. (Handwritten notes on the Greenfield family by G. M. A. Beck.) It was curiously fitting that George Garland, who rescued John Osborn Greenfield's Tales of Old Petworth from probable oblivion, should end his days in a property with which the author's grandfather John Greenfield had had such intimate association.

The White Hart public house which closed just before the outbreak of war in 1939 was socially very much a focal point for this part of Petworth, one or two of the local tradesmen being particular habitués. James Crow's 1779 Estate survey talks of "The sign of the Fighting Cocks with a shed and garden". The change of name to the White Hart is probably connected with the mid-nineteenth century switch that turned the Little White Hart in Middle Street into the present Red Lion. Between the wars the White Hart was the headquarters of Petworth Football Club and a noted centre for the ancient game of quoits, played on a separate piece of ground running alongside Rosemary Lane. Stan Adsett recalls, "The heavy rope rings were thrown with a distinctive backhanded flip and had to land on iron hooks positioned in the ground perhaps the length of a cricket pitch away. You can see that to play quoits a pub had to have a fair amount of space and not all pubs had this. The story goes that Harry Knight and some other men were playing quoits out of hours with a barrel of beer covered over beside them and Supt.

Gibbons, coming down the lane from the police station, looked over the fence as he passed. 'I shall be glad when it's opening time', volunteered Harry Knight. Supt. Gibbons must have had his doubts as to whether they were intending to wait that long! Quoits was a game for the older men and they didn't encourage youngsters to play" (*Petworth Society Bulletin* No. 58). At one side of the White Hart was the skittle room; Mr. Todman had the pub for much of the period between the wars.

The White Hart in late Victorian times was connected, as was the Queen's Head to the west, with the adjacent Stag Brewery run by the Milton family. Edwin Saunders writes: "In High Street there used to be a brewery. The man's name was Mr. Milton and beer used to be brewed there. That was done for a good many years. I used to have one of his gallon jars with his name on it. That was a big business years ago and all deliveries by horse and van". The premises may have been a brewhouse for some time: James Crow in 1779 speaks of a "house, malthouse stable and garden owned by Thomas Smith" in obvious proximity to the Fighting Cocks. Manning Milton appears to have taken over and expanded the business of his father Henry Milton, eventually taking his brother Henry, formerly a farmer at Lodsworth, into partnership with him. A Milton family tradition recalls that Henry "after visiting the fifty odd houses in the district supplied by the brewery, and after having had a sociable half-pint with each, would come home decidedly tipsy" (*Petworth Society Bulletin* No. 45). Manning Milton had eight children all of whom were to leave Petworth and almost all of whom were to die abroad. The family had all left Petworth by 1920.

Documents relating to the sale of the Stag Brewery and its satellites to Friary Holroyd and Healy the brewers in 1900 show that at this time Manning Milton's property stretched right along the south side of High Street from the White Hart to the Queen's Head. The many names of High Street caused problems even then. "When was East Street changed into High Street?" the purchaser's solicitors wanted to know. "We do not know when the change was made. The street has been known as Back Street or High Street for many years," was Brydone and Pitfield's reply to what they no doubt saw as legal nitpicking, (30th November 1899). The property at issue was extensive: there were more than a dozen cottages at the back of the Queen's Head while the White Hart also had five houses to the rear. The documents give some information on these: "The one nearest Red Lion Yard (i.e. the most westerly) was formerly Pullen and is now Mrs. Spooner's, the next has been unoccupied for some time, the next was Carters' and is now used as a malt-store, and the last on the right entering the yard and also fronting the High Street was Willmers and is now Woods."

Facing Middle Street is the unusual premises (now Chalcrafts) with the large room at the top. The sales particulars describe it as an artist's studio, "formerly a Club Room" but it is not now clear what its Victorian use as a Club Room would be, nor why such a large room should come into existence. The Daintrey family from East Street seem to have been renting it in 1900, Constance Daintrey being a painter of some distinction, noted for her rendering of local and continental scenes. The studio would revert to communal use in later years: for Mrs. Ford's "sixpenny hops" between the wars, dances during the war or Mrs. Frank Whitcomb's dancing classes after the war. At all times it was a well-known venue for whist drives, more frequent then than now. The loss of this room as a communal centre has taken some of the character from High Street. The small shop premises at the bottom were, according to the sales particulars, used as a spirit shop in 1900 and "entered from the cartway at the side". It is clear that the present entrance, restricted as it now seems, was used for access by the brewers' drays. In the 1930's Arthur Stevens conducted his boot-repair business from the shop.

The next two houses are described in 1900 as "fronting the High Street". First comes an eight-roomed cottage, brick and timber built and tiled, and then the Brewery House "of modern construction". The inference is that the house had been rebuilt by Manning Milton but this is not certain. In later years Mr. Spurgeon the vet would have the Brewery House and Mr. Murray, his assistant, the cottage to the east, both Mr. and Mrs. Spurgeon keeping hunters in the extensive outbuildings to the rear where the Stag Brewery had been. It is described in 1900 as a building to the rear with a cooling room on the second floor, and a mash room, refrigerator, and Tun Room and hop store on the first floor. On the ground floor was the brewery itself with coppers, hop rack, beer

High Street looking east. About 1900.

store and engine room. Whether the brewery continued to operate after Manning Milton sold it in 1900 and, if so for how long, is not at present possible to say. We can only re-echo Edwin Saunders and say, "that was a big business years ago".

The Queen's Head, with its cluster of small cottages to the south, formed the western boundary of Manning Milton's empire. In 1900 the pub was let out to Alfred Knowles "who has been in occupation for about fifteen years at the low rent of £15 per annum". The building in its present reconstructed form does not seem to go back beyond the mid-nineteenth century but a conveyance of 9th February 1887 from Mr. John Clue to Manning Milton writes of "All the messuage or tenements or beerhouse known by the name of the Queen's Head Inn and sometimes heretofore known by the sign of the Turk's Head Inn and sometimes formerly used as a wool warehouse and before that known as the Red Lion and anciently called Perkins".

This rubric clearly ranges over a long period. The old name "Perkins" has escaped even the scholarly annotator of the 1882 survey map and cannot at the other end of the time scale be picked up on John Ederton's 1541 return. The Red Lion too is very elusive as regards ancient record of it but was clearly once sufficiently dominating to give its name to the whole street. The street was Red Lion Street long before it was Back Street, let alone High Street. The 1882 survey locates the Red Lion marginally to the south of the Queen's Head premises. The old name of the Turk's Head survived in popular oral recollection as long as the Queen's Head itself survived as a pub. It was traditionally a beerhouse of the old-fashioned kind and its landlord needed, at least in the old days, a strong character. The Queen's Head catered for a somewhat robust clientele: cattle drovers snatching a night's rest before returning, itinerant peddlers, hawkers and entertainers, dossing down in the inn itself or sleeping rough in a shed at the back. There are still dim twice-told memories of boys creeping up to the back of the pub at dead of night to glimpse some exotic like a performing bear. Mrs. Henly was a notable landlady between the wars with the very necessary ability to impose order on those of her rough-hewn clients who failed to observe the not over-onerous proprieties of the house. Some idea of the cosmopolitan custom of the Queen's Head in mid-Victorian times is given by the census return of 1861. On the particular night of the census the Queen's Head housed four railway labourers with their wives and children, three single railway labourers, a saw sharpener and his wife, a general dealer, and six itinerant German musicians, all no doubt members of the same travelling band. The leader is 34 but of the other five, three are 16 years old, one 15 and one 14.

The sale documents speak of some fifteen cottages crammed into the tiny space at the back of the inn and contemporary plans show them extending southward in two long parallel lines. This was the Red Lion Yard. In the *Petworth Society Bulletin* No. 55 Dollie Mant recalls . . .

> "It was the custom for charity workers to be allotted a particular "district"; I think the Rector did this, and mother had the old Red Lion Yard as hers — a very populous area in those days. Taking on a "district" was no light matter although my mother seemed to have the light touch that was needed. A regular weekly visit, repeated over a period of years, meant that enduring friendships were formed. One family, I remember, always had a tart cooked for them, it was a regular weekly ritual. Mother never missed a weekly visit, knew who was ill, who needed help, how the children were getting on, in fact everything that a family friend would know. The Christmas when my father died he had bought blankets for Mother to give out to the "district" at Christmas but he said to her, "It's so cold, they ought to have them before Christmas"."

The cottages have now been pulled down for many years.

Knight's slaughter house was in the alley and there was stabling there too. George Payne speaks of sixteen to twenty hunters being kept there when he worked for Walter Dawtrey in Golden Square. Walter Dawtrey was a great aficionado of blood sports of all kinds and would keep the dogs up here in High Street overnight while the coursing meetings were being held on Frog Farm. As a boy Perce Durrant remembers occasionally being dispatched to the butchers for steak to feed the dogs. The houses to the west of the Queen's Head were not traditionally shops at all. Jeffrey Dawtrey, Walter's brother, lived in one that would become Biggs the butchers, while the house on the end of the row became Charles Leazell's office when he moved his builder's yard from Angel Street in the 1920s. Charles Leazell, the builder, was instrumental in converting private houses into shops and, on either side of the road, present-day High Street to an extent owes its present form to him. The next shop after the butcher's would be Dick Gale, the hairdresser's, afterward the quaintly named Chinese Lantern, a lending library run by Mrs. Card. Mrs. Palmer's little shop at the bottom of the row was not a conversion and has now reverted to being a private house. Mrs. Palmer is described as a greengrocer in Kelly's 1918 Directory but is better remembered as selling sweets or, on cold Sunday evenings, hot peppermint or blackcurrant cordial.

Between the Chinese Lantern and Mrs. Palmer's are a row of cottages (formerly Nos. 1-4 High Street) built on, or converted from, what had formerly been an ancient property known as Jervises tenement. The name is age-old and the origin unknown. WSRO Add. Ms. 275 carries the property, in some form at least, back to 1485 when one Richard Hoton gave it to fourteen named persons. After a brief mention in 1493 in the same source, Jervises disappears from view until 1674 when it was sold for £180 by Robert Warner to George Aylward and described as a "messuage, barn, backside and garden called Jervis in South Street, Petworth". Richard Kelly's tenement and garden lay to the west, and the tenement, backside and croft of Richard Robinson to south and east. This latter was clearly in multiple occupation; the tenants being named as Robert Warner, John James and Paul Harwood (O&A uncatalogued deeds). This latter property is clearly connected in some way with the ancient tenement of Barkers (shown in italics on the 1882 survey) with its satellite woodhouses adjoining or even forming part of it. George Aylward, a haberdasher, died in 1675 and his inventory lists six rooms, two cellars, a coalstore and a barn. John Aylward his son made several mortgages before selling eventually to Elizabeth Austen in 1710. Various changes follow which can be traced in PHA 863, 865 before in 1839 Jervises is described as part of Thomas Austin's property.

Archway House with its distinctive yard and equally distinctive archway, formed by bedrooms from adjoining cottages meeting overhead, is clearly of antiquity and character. The deeds, I am informed, do not carry the history back very far. Dr. Brydone

Mr. John Gallup. *Photograph by George Garland. Garland Collection.*

writing in the late 1940s relates, "Mr. Austin, the exciseman, bought the ground behind the Archway and tucked into the space his last home about 150 years ago. He had his office underneath the archway. His third wife was so fond of asparagus that the little garden on the south side was just one big asparagus bed". One can only wonder what source Dr. Brydone had for this information, apparently oral but stretching back such a very long time. Certainly I have never seen any sign of written confirmation of all this but the mention of Thomas Austin must prevent a hasty rejection of this tradition; he is known to have had the property in 1839.

A notable occupant of Archway House between the wars was Colonel Mayne, a military gentleman of autocratic manner. He had a little dog whose daily walks had about them a military precision as to time that did credit to his master's soldierly background. In wartime when his daughter lived at Archway, the space under the archway was the venue for the ancestor of the present WI market in the Leconfield Hall, the WI bringing all their spare vegetables to Archway House. Lady Shakerley recalls, "The gate was opened up, and fair weather or foul, the vegetables were sold under the arch. I well remember the beetroot and the beans, but there were all sorts of things on the big trestle table under the arch. Whatever was left over the Army would buy for the camps" (*Petworth Society Bulletin* No. 56).

# 12

## GOLDEN SQUARE

WHY GOLDEN Square? John Ederton's 1541 return makes no mention of such a place and it is probable that at this time it was considered an appendage of Market Square. Atthall (now Whitehall) in Golden Square is described in a Petworth House deed of the time as "alias Hall Place in Market Place". An old name is the Beast Market and the new name of Golden Square has no discernible historical basis. One wonders who dreamed up the new name and how quickly it triumphed over the old. So complete is the victory of the new however that it would require a certain sophistication now to know what was meant by the Beast Market. The change would seem to be due not only to the decline of the weekly market held here at one time but also to the desire to bury a homespun past rather in the manner that wealthy merchants would disguise the timber fronts of their houses with a Georgian brick façade. We may guess that the Causey became Lombard Street and Back Street High Street for similar reasons of propriety. Golden Square is withdrawn a few yards from the through traffic that streams endlessly down New Street and stands perpetually in the shadow of Market Square to which it looks slightly up, and from which the traffic divides it. This does not seem to give Golden Square a sense of inferiority: on the contrary it pulses with a character of its own. No doubt it has always done so.

The shopping arcade with its office and business premises may be new but the site is age-old. The more colloquial "bunhouse", originally applied to the bakers on the west side of Market Square, has been replaced by the "Old Bakery", like the Beast Market a sacrifice on the altar of respectability. Who ever heard of a development called the "Old Bunhouse"? In fact the old Granary might be a more accurate title for here, as the century turned, was a large grain store. A huge wooden board, visible only from certain vantage points, sturdily proclaims the name of Dawtrey the grain-merchants still. The board is truly a survivor and would need a degree of determination to remove it. Long may it remain to set the enquiring eye to wonder about Petworth as once it was!

Ernest Carver recalled working as a boy at Parkhurst Farm, Upperton before the Great War. Mr. Brittain was the farmer there then. Walter Dawtrey the grain merchant would send two men up to Parkhurst to cut and tie a hay-rick and Ernest would deliver it to Dawtrey's cornstore, a ton and a half at a load. Three horses were needed to pull the cart, working in trace harness, one behind the other. Even with a good horse in front it was difficult to get them into the yard, but once they were in, the bales would be thrown off the waggon and hauled up into the store with a kind of grab.

Walter Dawtrey had stabling in Golden Square for some eight to ten hunters, letting them out for hire. The stable wall remains, backing on to the lane that runs to the side. The rest of the premises appear to have been used by the granary business. Another sixteen to twenty hunters were kept in stables near the Queen's Head in High Street. The horses were thorough-breds bought personally by Walter Dawtrey on periodic visits to Ireland. George Payne, who worked there as a youngster, helped to muck out the horses, exercise and groom them, taking them out two at a time, one ridden and one led.

While he had found it necessary to venture into the world of commerce, Walter Dawtrey was well aware of his ancient lineage and his family's long history in the locality. As befits perhaps a lineage of such antiquity he is remembered as being somewhat peremptory. The correspondent in Views and Reviews pays as much attention to the Dawtrey pedigree as he does to the grain business: indeed so keen is he to extol the Dawtrey name that his first sentence all but succumbs altogether in a welter of subordinate clauses! The Dawtreys were never of course lords of Petworth but of neighbouring Moor, so near, yet so distant away over the fields. Mr. Dawtrey certainly seems here to be having the best of all worlds — a man of business who has yet not forfeited the respect due to his ancient line.

MR. WALTER DAWTREY, MALTSTER, CORN, SEED AND COAL MERCHANT, GOLDEN SQUARE, PETWORTH.

No Sussex man will for a moment deny that there are many good and sufficient reasons for asserting that any historical or descriptive sketch of Petworth, as we find it at the present day, would possess any claim to completeness that omitted to include a review of the business carried on by the above mentioned gentleman, who represents a line of honourable ancestry reaching backward as far as the Norman invasion, and containing in its long roll the names of warriors, statesmen and even a Lord High Chancellor of England. The Dawtrey family came over with the Conqueror, and after the decisive battle of Hastings, 1066, became settled on lands granted by the king to the family, and situate at Petworth, of which, until late in the 18th century, the Dawtreys were Lords of the Manor. Circumstances, however, over which the present head of the house had no control, have rendered it incumbent that further distinctions for the family could only be sought in the arena of commercial enterprise, and with a courage that certainly has not been weakened by good breeding, Mr. Walter Dawtrey commenced business some years ago as a maltster, corn, seed and coal merchant, right in the very heart of the country which his long line of forefathers lorded it over for many generations. Mr. Dawtrey enjoys a valuable connection throughout the district, and in all departments of his business he endeavours to meet the requirements of his customers with promptitude, and in a manner that shall not do discredit to the honourable name he honourably bears. Excellent facilities are enjoyed for the expeditious fulfilment of all contracts and heavy stocks are held to meet local demands. As a capable farmer, holding land under the Right Honourable Lord Leconfield, Mr. Dawtrey is well known, and he enjoys a wide reputation as a thorough sportsman, taking an active part in the runs of the neighbouring packs of fox and staghounds, notably with the Lord Leconfield's, the Crawley and Horsham, the Southdown and the Warnham staghounds. Mr. Dawtrey deals extensively in first rate hunters, of which he is recognised as an experienced judge. He receives the most liberal support at the hands of the leading families in this part of the county. Long experience and a perfect knowledge both of equine and general agricultural matters have enabled Mr. Dawtrey to achieve an especially high degree of success in meeting the requirements of a distinguished *clientele*, and his business may be considered an important adjunct of Petworth's commercial and industrial activity. The telegraphic address is "Dawtrey, Petworth."

Some of the old granary premises were used at various times by other local businesses, a baker operating on the ground floor for many years. Upstairs, in the early years after the Great War, an exiled Londoner, Mr. Johnson, worked as a rulemaker. Johnson was one of the very last craftsmen to make rules by hand and examples of his work still survive. Lancewood, the hardest wood known at the time, was a staple material and the wood was planed into shape from the rough, sand-papered, french-polished and cut to size. There were no power tools then. Surveyors' rods were a speciality, three foot or five foot in length with a spring clip in the middle. Other items were school rulers, T-Squares and spirit-levels. All were stamped with Mr. Johnson's stamp. Bill Payne who worked there as an apprentice for four years after leaving school, started at five shillings a week but came in the end to earn a full guinea a week. He says, "I believe that we were almost the last doing this work by hand. Machines were taking over and we could not compete pricewise with them though our products were far better" (*Petworth Society Bulletin* No. 44). One of the perks of a job at Mr. Johnson's was a supply of free cakes from the baker's downstairs!

The buildings have had all sorts of uses over the years, some chronicled, some, we may be sure, beyond the reach of even the most tenuous retrospect. At the close of the last century a part of the complex, just a room perhaps at the rear, was used as a Gentleman's Club, known as the Rooks' Club after an ancient name for the property. Rooks was a place where professional men could meet for billiards, a chat, a look at the newspaper and particularly, one would suppose, for a drink. Applications to join were carefully monitored by the committee. The Rooks' Club was never probably very numerous but it guarded its social status jealously, being confined to professional men like the doctors, the bank manager, the more socially aware businessmen and of course those who had no need to indulge in commerce at all. Some accounts remain from the mid 1880s and early 1890s but the Rooks' Club probably did not survive until the century turned. Mr. Otway the landlord

The sitting room at Moor Farm in 1894. The elaborate ceiling would later be put up in Lancaster House but has since disappeared. *Photograph by Walter Kevis. Garland Collection.*

complained to the gentlemen of the Rooks' Club in February 1888 of the late hours they, his tenants, were keeping, to the considerable annoyance of his other tenants in adjacent properties. Exclusiveness has never been a guarantee of ordered behaviour. In a letter to Mr. Otway the chastised gentlemen of the Club expressed their indignation at these "false and exaggerated" reports but, with somewhat bad grace, regretted any undue noise. They would take care that the nuisance did not occur again.

Facing one as one looks down from the Market Square is Lancaster House, still an imposing building and originally, one would certainly imagine, one big house. It has long been partitioned: L. C. Barnes, writing in 1902, knew of the property being divided into Lancaster House on the right while "through an archway, leading into a tiny paved courtyard, is York House". Dr. Brydone, writing for the Women's Institute Scrapbook in the 1940s, calls the whole property "York and Lancaster House" and says that it has been a private house and inn "where (it is said) visitors' servants from Petworth House were sent to lodge". The qualifying phrase "it is said", indicates a certain unease on Dr. Brydone's part, but rather less unease than "they say". The courtyard might well suggest an inn; but equally the presence of the yard might just as easily lead someone to suggest an inn when none was there. Miss Beck (*Inns and Alehouses*) sites no inn here but as she would be the first to admit, her list is not exhaustive and some short-lived hostelries like the Bell or the Anchor seem never to have been formally identified. The small walled gardens to the north of Lancaster House are unusual too, the doors opening into Rosemary Lane and the effect reminding Mrs. Barnes of the city walls of Chichester. Dr. Brydone thought the steep artificial banks in these gardens had once held wine-cellars, while others have thought of ice-houses. "They say," Dr. Brydone continues, obviously feeling on rather uncertain ground, "that in Cromwellian times the beautiful communion plate from St. Mary's Church was hidden in the garden of York and Lancaster House. The house was sold and the new tenant found the treasure and sold it for his own profit". The bulk of the present church plate is certainly later, being the gift of Dr. Price the rector in 1665, but whether this is enough to validate this tradition is another matter.

Lancaster House in 1934. A pencil drawing by Charles Leazell.

For such an important property these wisps of tradition are a very thin harvest. Some indication of earlier owners might give further clues and such indication may eventually be forthcoming. Even the earliest photographs show the shop existing much as it does now, although doubtless there was originally a house front. Mrs. Burnett's toy and fancy goods repository moved to Golden Square from Rectory Gate in the mid-nineteenth century. Ernest Streeter started his antique business in this shop, and of late years the Haslemere Co-operative Society had a branch here. Walter Dawtrey lived for many years at Lancaster House and Mrs. Barnes records that when Moor Farm was rebuilt by the Leconfield Estate, "Lord Leconfield the owner gave the handsome old oak carving with which it was decorated to Mr. Walter Dawtrey who has put it up in Lancaster House". The carving referred to is a beautifully fashioned wooden ceiling and a photograph of it in its old home survives from 1894. The fate of the panelling is unknown. Some say it went to America. Certainly it is no longer at Lancaster House. The old manor house of Moor had been largely demolished in 1763 and converted into a farm-house. In 1786 it had been sold to Lord Egremont by the Bishop of Llandaff to whom it had been bequeathed.

In older days Petworth Fair extended into Golden Square and the Square stood in a manner on the very periphery of the town abutting effectively on the border of the garden land that extended south to Station Road. Valerian grows in the walls of Back Lane, a sign, some say, that the Romans were once here, but Petworth is not in fact a Roman settlement. Rosemary Gardens, like the land to the east, were once allotments and the Gardens still provide a refuge for some of the old trees, secure at last we may suppose from the ravages of the developer. Further down, over what is now the wall of the car park, a mulberry tree would drop its pippy, pulpy, fruit to lie in the rough gutter of the lane. A Petworth shibboleth if you like: the town dividing sharply into those who remember the mulberry tree and those who do not. Popular tradition says that the long high walls of the Back Lane once guarded prisoners being led down from the Gaol to the Pound for execution. We may be pleased that the truth is more prosaic: Petworth was never, as far as I know, host to such dismal rites. In a wasteland of cars the high walls are simply a reminder of a forgotten paradise of walled gardens.

On the west side of Golden Square a single building with a brick façade houses three business premises and has done so now for many years. In the nineteenth century, by contrast, the whole building was a single shop and its proprietor Benjamin Challen is commemorated still by the letters BC clearly visible on the top storey. The brick façade, as often in Petworth, covers a much older timber framing. An invoice of 1846 proclaims the firm of Benjamin Challen to be tea-dealers, grocers and importers of Irish provisions, maltsters and spirit merchants, and office of the Norwich Union Fire and Life Assurance. Coffee was roasted on the premises on "the most approved principles".

Benjamin Challen however was far more than a grocer and his spirit still seems in quieter moments to pervade the Square and give it its peculiar feel. While Market Square has always looked toward St. Mary's for spiritual succour, Golden Square has over two centuries looked to the non-conforming cause. Long before the Congregationalists built their chapel in the 1850s their cousins the Independents had a chapel in Golden Square, a direct ancestor, as we have seen, of the Ebenezer in Back Road. The chapel was registered with the Bishop of Chichester in March 1828, the application being signed by three Benjamin Challens, grandfather, father and son, William Gathercole the minister, William Nightingale a carpenter, Benjamin Rothwell a collarmaker and William Thorp a clerk. The Providence Chapel as it would be called, was a place of some considerable size, seating some two hundred persons, and under the guidance of the second Benjamin Challen a venue for distinguished preachers of the Independent cause. The chapel survived at least until the death of the second Benjamin Challen in 1867 but it has disappeared now as if it had never been. All remembrance, even of the site, is lost. Some think it was on the top floor of the Challens' shop premises and in truth it is difficult to see where else it could have been. It does seem however a curious place for a chapel and it is not easy to reconcile such a long room with apparently older features of the building. Be this as it may, Golden Square, in the middle years of the nineteenth century, would have echoed and re-echoed with the sound of the Independents singing. The Independent cause, like that of the

Presbyterians before them, was one of the smaller tradesmen and craftsmen in the larger towns — Petworth was "large" by nineteenth century Sussex standards — and Golden Square was indeed for them "an abiding city".

The main source for this lost world is a volume of sermons preached in the Providence Chapel at Petworth and in other places by James Hallett formerly of Alfriston, then of Mayfield, a prominent and eloquent Independent preacher of the time. Of the eighteen sermons, each separately printed but now bound together to form a single volume, ten are preached at Providence Chapel Petworth, two at Midhurst, two in Nottingham and one each at Chichester, Sunderland, Coventry and Bedford. Sunderland's Jireh Chapel seems a long way away and reflects no doubt the coming of the railways rather than the travelling on horseback that earlier preachers like John Wesley had so painfully made. A number of the Petworth sermons come from the spring of 1849, Monday evening being a popular time. On Good Friday in that year Mr. Hallett preached twice in the Providence Chapel, morning and afternoon. The sermons are a biblical mosaic; powerfully argued and delivered no doubt with considerable power. Personal details are very few and the last sermon in the book, preached at Petworth on January 13th 1867 marks the end of an era, the death of the second Benjamin Challen. Mr. Hallett's sabbath morning text is: "Mark the perfect man, and behold the upright: for the end of that man is peace." (Psalms 37:37). Benjamin Challen, we are told, had been called by grace under the ministry of the late Mr. Parsons, one time pastor at the Zion Chapel at Chichester, during the time that he was preaching at Minstead near Midhurst. Up to that time Challen had been in his own words "both in and out of the world". "At that time one branch of his business led him very much into worldly society, which after grace had reached his heart, he could not conscientiously carry on; and to avoid the snare and put a stop to the temptation, he disposed of that part of his business and came out from amongst them." James Hallett is presumably talking of the licensed portion of the business. Hallett and Challen had first met at Chichester in the autumn of 1844 and after that first meeting Challen would frequently drive the twenty-two miles to Bolney where Hallett preached once a month on the sabbath to hear him. "I question if

Damer's Bridge in the 1920s. *Photograph by George Garland. Garland Collection.*

the union and affection that existed between David and Jonathan was stronger than our own love to each other." The congregation have lost a good and faithful friend. "One who felt great interest in your welfare both in temporal and spiritual things: in the course of truth in this place he took the greatest interest, from the time the Lord called him by his grace, up to the time of his death, and as you know, it was supported principally by him. And occasionally did he invite men of God from a distance to preach to you, wholly at his own expense; and being blessed with a good understanding and judgement in the truth, he brought sterling men of truth to you. His motto was not to invite any minister until he had heard him with satisfaction."

The loss of Benjamin Challen was a body blow from which the Independent cause never recovered. The business passed eventually into other hands and the chapel was lost. Messrs. Jukes were the grocers there by the late 1870s and after them Otways. The present division into three shops comes from early this century. Benjamin Challen's empire, spiritual and material, is as if it had never been. His memorial remains, as it should be, his best friend's eulogy of him: "I can but speak highly of his character, and would not extol the creature, a worm of the dust, a sinner saved by grace, but extol the Saviour, and the richness, freeness and abounding of His grace!"

On the eastern side of the Square is the imposing building that now houses the Midland Bank. Part of the premises are still in private use. Petworth House deeds going back to medieval times associate the house with the Hall family and the old name is Attehall or, occasionally, Hall's Place. A later use of the site was for the Star Inn and Miss Beck (*Inns and Alehouses* p. 142) knows of a licence "to keep the Starr" granted to Nicholas Turgis in 1618. There seems no mention of Attehall in John Ederton's 1541 return but Rose Turges has a messuage in the Market Place called Avenynges and an easement to build to the south and west of her tenement. This may well carry Rose Turges in the direction of Attehall but it is difficult to be precise. Of the later history of the site little is known and it is one of the few places in Petworth of which no ancient photograph survives. Mr. Thomas Sherwin, formerly of Moor, was living at Whitehall in the 1870s, while Kelly's Directory for 1918 gives Mrs. Violet Bromham, antique dealer, as having the commercial premises. Bromhams had dealt in furniture for some years. It is not clear what changes were made when the premises changed hands. Whitehall on the face of it appears a simple corruption of Attehall.

The present bank seems to have started off as three rooms in Whitehall, the Bromham shop facing out on to High Street rather than Golden Square. Tradition has it that the bank's foundation came about through Mr. Podmore from Newlands complaining in London about the lack of local banking facilities and, as a shareholder, being in a position to get something done about it. "We'll make sure you receive better service than this" was the reply his protest elicited and the three rooms were the bank's initial response.

Damer's Bridge with its strange high pavement and disordered diamond-etched paving stones still carries the name of the Dammer family, saddlers here in the eighteenth century. The bridge is a reference to the open sewer that ran down roughly where the Car Park entrance now is. Damer's Bridge was a popular haunt for George Garland between the wars, a vista of cobble and gable that time, it seemed, had passed by. With the Car Park entrance having taken out the last house on the south side, the impression now is more of a row of teeth after an extraction. An older name is Sowter Ditch, shown in the 1882 map as an archaic name and clearly mentioned by John Ederton in 1541. John Polyng has a cottage near the forge and by Sowter's Dyche while John Davye has a parcel of land lying over against the Sowter Dyche called Chechebotes, thirty feet by sixteen feet. The forge may well be roughly where the Tudor Cottage restaurant is now, the early nineteenth century Churchwardens' Vestry Book speaks of a forge there being removed to facilitate the passage of traffic. Old deeds refer to this area as the Bull Corner. Chechebotes is difficult now to identify.

The site of the present United Reformed Church seems to have been old cottages, Damer's Bridge with houses on either side being perhaps rather less of a backwater then than now. A lane up through toward the present Star Inn was known as Four Corner Alley because of the meeting of four corners of different properties at one point along its length.

While in the early nineteenth century Golden Square was a

stronghold of the nonconforming faith, the most lasting expression of that faith, the present United Reformed Church, was not built until the late 1850s. For a while the Congregational chapel, as it then was, and the Providence Chapel must have co-existed, both descendents of that same Presbyterian movement that had suffered so much in earlier centuries to expiate its brief period of ascendancy during the Commonwealth. Arnold's *History* (1864) does not mention the new chapel at all nor, except in passing, does Mrs. Barnes in 1902, but the United Reformed Church with its Hall has been for years a focus of Petworth life in general, not simply that of the church itself. The wooden spire that once would have seemed unassuming in comparison with the lordly spire of St. Mary's has now survived its august counterpart by two generations. Atmospheric pollution has had some effect, particularly on the local stone used on parts of the building but extensive renovation has been carried out recently. Of the history of the church from its establishment and of its previous wanderings the church's own records must speak. The United Reformed Church, unlike the Providence Chapel, still has a living tradition of its own that can speak for it.

Avenings is a house dating in its present form perhaps to the mid-eighteenth century but the name is certainly much older than this, occurring as we have seen already in the 1541 return. A quitrent receipt from 1820 describes Avenings as formerly Sadlers, once Comptons and late Mary Woolgar's, the last name taking us back at least as far as the Window Tax Return of 1762, the others certainly much further. In the early nineteenth century Avenings was the home of the Palmer family. Robert Rice Palmer, a wealthy mercer, died in 1829 but his widow survived him at Avenings a good fifteen years. The Palmer family had, as we have seen, some connection with Pettifers in Church Street at the close of the eighteenth century. Robert Rice Palmer had been treasurer of the Petworth Turnpike Road until 1816 and lived at Avenings in some style, renting a number of outlying farms from the Leconfield Estate, Montpelier in the Gog, nearby Brinksole, Gunter's Bridge on the road to Balls Cross and the land east of the Pound in Station Road that would later become allotments. The Palmers with their small rented farms presided over a kind of alternative Leconfield

Estate but on a much smaller scale: a Leconfield Estate in microcosm. Surviving invoices show that the Palmers' farming venture was an important source of employment for local tradesmen, particularly in maintenance on rented farms and cottages. In the 1830s and 1840s Mrs. Palmer made significant use of the local carriers for bringing luxury goods from London, making particular use of William Collins. For a small charge Collins would bring the goods and pay the invoice for her in London. Lavender water from Fisher Toller and Co. of Hanover Square, perfume from John Gosnell and Co. of Lombard Street in the City, bread and biscuits from Lemanns the French bread and Fancy Biscuit maker in Threadneedle Street, tea and spices from Davison and Newman of 44 Fenchurch Street, a barrel of oysters from Messrs. Wise the fishmongers of Ludgate Hill are just a few of the wares brought over a period to Avenings. On Mrs. Palmer's death the house would pass to Mrs. Blagden her daughter, along with the considerable Palmer wealth.

In the early years of the 1914-18 war, Avenings by now occupied by the Mant family, had soldiers of the Rifle Brigade billeted there and occupying the entire top storey. There were thirty-six men in all, twenty-four in one room and twelve in the other. They stayed for some three months on either side of Easter 1915 and always referred to Petworth as "Wetworth" because it seemed to be forever raining.

A particular feature of Avenings in the period up to the war, and also after it, was the Mants' annual jumble sale held in the garden. Dollie Mant recalled (*Petworth Society Magazine* No. 55) . . .

"It was in aid of Pearson's Fresh Air Fund, a charity for city children who would not normally have a holiday. The Fund sent them away to the seaside or into the country. As such things often do, the Jumble Sale had started in a small, almost casual, way. One year we ourselves didn't go on holiday but were given two shillings and sixpence each which we used to buy items for a bran-tub for the Pearson's Fund. It was very successful but we soon learned that if you had said the Sale was for Pearson's Fund then all the money had to go to that particular fund. As we wanted to make some of the money over to local charities we had to advertise the Sale in future years as "in aid of the Pearson Fresh Air Fund and other objects".

The Sale, as I have said, was held in the garden at Avenings and it was open to everyone. It became, over the years, something of an institution. One year Mary Pickford the film-star was in England and donated a gold watch to whoever gave the biggest subscription to the Pearson Fund while she was here. Our Jumble Sale happened to be early that year and we won the gold watch; my niece still has it."

Messrs. Jukes, Golden Square about 1880. *Photograph by Walter Kevis. Garland Collection.*

# 13

## MARKET SQUARE

IT WOULD hardly be helpful to say that Market Square is not a street because it is a Square: it is, of course, both. As Petworth's premier street, it can also be considered its most ancient. If we could be sure that Market Square has always been the venue for Petworth's ancient November fair "in the feast of St. Edmund the king" we could carry the story back to 1273 but at this distance in time we are moving in a very uncertain world.

What we can however certainly say is that, by the time of John Ederton's 1541 return of rents to his master Henry VIII, some of the most ancient Market Square sites already have their historic names. William Young's "messuage with a croft belonging to it called Serles, once Agnes Berkford's" is a time-honoured designation of the ancient site that would later form part of the Swan Inn in the south-west corner of the Square. John Turgys' tenement called Telyngs still survives in name at least, while Thomas Telyng's messuage and garden called Mewys is on the present National Westminster Bank site. Henry Ubley's messuage called Dorunts lay in part across the present junction with New Street and would be truncated to accommodate that very newest of Petworth's old streets. Thomas Vyvyan's Belchambers, later the White Hart Inn, lay on the site of the present Austens. Rose Turges' Avenyngs is very modern sounding but should sound a note of caution. At a distance of some four hundred and fifty years, coincidence of name may well signify identity of site but far less likely identity of structure. Not all Ederton's property names can be elucidated. Where for instance was Thomas Portbury's "Wylmers" or Thomas Telyng's tenement called "Sladys" in the Market Place?

John Ederton mentions stalls in the market such as those of James Turges "late William Rykford's and before that William Fourd's and once John Neles" and it may be that already by 1541 there was an open Market House with stalls on the site of the present Leconfield Hall. Clearly over the centuries the Market House was an integral part of Petworth's corporate life and the hub of the ancient office of Portreeve or clerk of the market. Its history, as is the nature of such buildings, is assumed rather than recorded. Echoes of its demolition can be picked up in PHA 2233, accounts for the building of the new hall in 1793. The raising of the new and the removal of the old seem to have been different facets of a roughly simultaneous process. The new building cost £184.6.6d. and was paid for by the Third Earl of Egremont, the stone and wood coming of course from the Estate.

There was a courtroom on the upper floor of the new hall, and facility for a weekly Saturday market on the ground floor, much as there had been in the old Market House. Petty Sessions were held twice monthly and at Epiphany and Easter the upstairs rooms played host to the County Quarter Sessions. According to the *Tales of Old Petworth* (pp.44-5) the Third Earl of Egremont would very occasionally allow visiting players use of the hall and on even rarer occasions grace their performance with his own presence. Extensive alterations in 1864 and 1869 converted the downstairs part into rooms to be used for "mental recreation and improvement", and it may well be that the lectures on which Arnold's *History* is based owe their origin to the educational impetus fostered by these changes. Two old houses adjoining the Town Hall to the north-west were pulled down at this time (PHA 4876). Further alterations were made in 1891.

At the turn of the century the Town Hall was the responsibility of a commissionaire, the best-known holder of the post being Sgt. Avent, a retired military man. Not only had he to keep the Hall cleaned and ready for entertainments, council meetings, court sessions and the like, but also to act as messenger at the Leconfield Estate office when not otherwise engaged. A curious sideline was his duty to show the pictures at Petworth House on Tuesdays and Thursdays if so required. Arthur Beckett (*The Wonderful Weald* 1911 p. 341) recalled a visit to see the pictures, arriving at Petworth House five minutes before the hour of opening. "We were ushered into a long, bare, barrack-like room with rows of chairs, set against the walls, on which about a dozen persons, visitors like ourselves, were seated. On the striking of eleven there entered into the room an old soldier wearing medals. He conducted us to a little office where we visitors signed our names and the number of persons in our respective parties . . . Then after our ex-soldier guide we trooped . . . through room after room containing hundreds of pictures, pieces of antique furniture and specimens of carving by Grinling Gibbons."

A great change in the historic role of the Town Hall came with the construction of the Iron Room to the rear of the present National Westminster Bank. The large corrugated temporary structure had been raised to allow church services to be held during extensive renovations to St. Mary's Church. These renovations were completed in 1904 but, as is the way of such things, the Iron Room remained in being and functionary for some sixty years after this, its first purpose, had been fulfilled. The Iron Room was to take a great deal of pressure from the Town Hall as (with the possible exception of the Swan Ballroom) the only centre for live entertainment in Petworth. Writing to an applicant for use of the Town Hall in 1906 Herbert Watson, land agent to the Leconfield Estate, put the new situation succinctly enough: "The Iron Room is larger and much more convenient for concerts than the Town Hall". The Iron Room was in Lord Leconfield's gift as was the Town Hall and the ownership of the two halls gave Lord Leconfield an effective if not perhaps always consciously realized monopoly of what Petworth had offered it in the way of entertainment. Herbert Watson or one of his successors would pass on any letter of application to his Lordship who would return it marked "Yes. L." or "No. L." usually without other comment. There was no appeal. The halls were let (or not let) by his Lordship: he had decided and that was that.

Dramatic entertainments basically needed a licence from the magistrates but there was an uneasy borderline as to what actually constituted a theatre play. Miss Elson, head mistress of the East Street Girls' School, while a model of propriety in other ways, rode this border territory with magisterial abandon. "I think Miss Elson sails very close to the wind in not getting a licence for her entertainment", wrote Herbert Watson to Mr. Penrose the Rector in November 1906. The Iron Room was capable of holding much larger audiences than the Town Hall, an early century cinematograph entertainment packed in several hundred, but it was not until the early 1930s that it was finally licensed for stage plays. The Iron Room was demolished in 1963, becoming a car standing before it was finally developed as it is at present.

Between these two axes of Lord Leconfield's spiritual control lay the Half Moon Inn, on the site now occupied by the present National Westminster Bank. Formerly a copyhold called Mewes or Mewys, the beginnings of the inn go back at least to Edward Martin in the early seventeenth century (Lord Leconfield, *Petworth Manor* p. 125). PHA 3955 reports that a succeeding tenant, Thomas Moody, was presented before the manorial court in September 1666 for laying stones and timber in the Market Place and given until the 20th of the month to remove them under pain of being fined ten shillings. In April 1674 Moody was allowed by the court to run a lead pipe into the upper conduit near the church stile to convey water into a cistern in his yard "beinge the signe of the Half Moon Inn Petworth," subject to other inhabitants having access to the cistern.

The inn was purchased by the Duke of Somerset in 1712 and would appear during the eighteenth century to have been the most prosperous of the Market Square inns. Sold by the Earl of Egremont in 1785 it was repurchased by him in 1812. The 1812 fixture list survives, speaking among other items of a bar, "the engine that drives the beer from the cellar" and a new smoke jack. The last was a device for turning a roasting spit in a chimney, making use of the rising gases. There was, too, a kitchen range and a copper fixed behind the chimney jamb.

Late nineteenth century photographs show an attractive creeper-covered building as befits the characteristically mellow epitaph that appears in *Views and Reviews* . . .

"HALF MOON," OLD ESTABLISHED FAMILY HOTEL, MRS. PYECROFT, PROPRIETRESS, ALSO OF THE SWAN HOTEL, PETWORTH.

The "Half Moon" hotel is one of those picturesque, old established hostelries at which it is the delight of strangers to England, especially Americans, to sojourn. There is a soothing charm in the double-storeyed gables which is irresistible, and the unpretentious quietness which prevails, as compared with our modern innovations, is at once restful and an assurance of the solid comforts to be found within. The "Half Moon" is the hotel *par excellence* of Petworth, and has for many years enjoyed its present reputation. It is a most familiar landmark to the residents, situated as it is in the immediate vicinity of the Market Square, Town Hall and the time honoured Petworth House; and there are hundreds throughout the country who doubtless recall with pleasurable memories the undisturbed sleep enjoyed under its hospitable roof, and also the good old time dishes which are a feature of its cuisine. All the rooms are handsomely furnished, and there is in evidence on all sides, the fact that every care has been bestowed on making the guests comfortable and at ease in its luxurious surroundings. On the ground floor is a coffee-room of the good old fashioned sort and a ladies' drawing-room, while on the floor above are the sitting and bed-rooms, all well appointed, thoroughly ventilated, light and cheerful. The cellars, away below, contain a fine stock of choice old wines of noted vintages, a fact which can be vouched for by the numerous visitors who make the "Half Moon" their resting place while in town for the purpose of inspecting the fine, old picture gallery for which Petworth House is famous. An omnibus from the hotel meets all trains, and parties desiring to travel any distance will find the hotel of the greatest convenience, for special attention is given to posting in all its branches.

The new bank building designed by Frederick Wheeler in the Edwardian Baroque style and roofed with Horsham stone dates from the turn of the century.

On the Park Road corner lay Baxter's Smithy, still remembered as a going concern by so many local people, Mr. Baxter looking out of the forge to see if anyone was coming. The forge lay at the front with the shoeing shed to the rear and the shoeing yard right at the back. To the south lay the great mass of the Iron Room.

The present bank has a garden to the east, once the site of a watchmaker's shop. The name Teelings for the property to the east of the garden goes back certainly to the early seventeenth century, perhaps even before, but in the sixteenth century it is the Turges family who are intimately connected with this site. PHA 7362 mentions Thomas Turges' fair house as "standing in Petworth Market Place over against the place where the courte was keapte" and it was the dispute over copyhold fines on this particular property that sparked off the long legal battle between Henry Percy, Ninth Earl of Northumberland, and his tenants over copyhold law.

The site appears to have been redeveloped by Richard Stokes in the early seventeenth century to accommodate an eating-house knwon as the Parlour and several shops. Richard Stokes' daughter Benedicta Ayre kept up the eating-house and added an ale-house at the rear of the Half Moon that would later be known as the Ship. By the late century John Snagge the "medician" had his premises here as too did Thomas Willis the mercer who would eventually purchase most of the copyhold. Lord Leconfield (*Petworth Manor* pp. 121ff) gives the seventeenth century history of the property in some detail but can offer little on its history over the next one hundred and fifty years. By the turn of the present century the shop had become Nevatts the tailors, other long-standing occupiers, Major Syer, Mr. Standen and Mr. Wakeford all following the same trade.

Master Nevatt's massive ledger survives as a passport to a late Victorian and Edwardian world that is gone — a world of spats, cycling suits, straw hats, astrakhan gloves and, in 1903, Mr. Otway's motoring cap! The business clearly existed, as businesses did then, on a veritable spider's web of credit, quite substantial sums always being outstanding and paid with no great urgency, at least as it appears now to a financially more stringent age. Very occasionally, and only after an interminable period, would Master Nevatt mark up the despairing words "Bad debt". These seem usually to have been relatively trifling amounts.

Teelings is not mentioned by Mr. Greenfield in the *Tales* but he does know of one Mr. Robert Upperton "a draper who lived in Mr. Jupp's house recently pulled down and replaced by Messrs. Eager and Lewis". The property is now shared between Davids and Morris Antiques. Pigot's 1826 Directory lists Robert Upperton as a "wool-stapler," basically a middle-man or grader of wool. A predecessor here was almost certainly Benjamin Faulconer the mercer, the house being then known rather confusingly as Trump Alley (see G. M. A. Beck in Kenyon, *Town and Trades* p. 112). It was a large house returning 23 windows for tax purposes in 1762. The Eager family were to continue as drapers here for generations.

MARKET SQUARE

The north side of Market Square about 1885. Teelings on the right appears still to be a private house. The clockmakers on the left may have been demolished with the Half Moon Inn in 1899. *Photograph by Walter Kevis. Garland Collection.*

The same return gives Mr. Whicher as having the present solicitors' premises, returning nineteen windows in 1762. The stopped windows looking sightlessly out over the Market Square are a memorial now to this forgotten tax. Although a commercial premises for generations the property appears never formally to have been converted to shop use.

Tradition has it that here was the first home of the old-established Petworth bookselling and printing business operated first by James Goldring, then by John Phillips and lastly by Phillips' son-in-law Albert Bryant. Alan Bryant, writing in the *Sussex County Magazine* in December 1931 prints a late Victorian photograph of the press at work and discusses a file of proofs from 1813 "each proof bearing on the back the name of the person for whom it was done, the number printed and the price". Auction sheets, sales catalogues, rate collection forms and notices of articles lost and rewards offered are staple productions. We may assume that just a single random year's proofs had been kept and the others destroyed. We may wonder too what happened to Alan Bryant's treasures and the photograph he had of the press at work. Bryants would move later to the west corner of the churchyard and finally to East Street. A Victorian photograph perhaps from the 1870s shows the house as apparently a tailor's; the ubiquitous name Nevatt appears in the window and amazingly there is no sign of the famous wisteria. Old prints show the Regency lamp in its full glory but now only the lamp-bracket remains, discernible by the determined amongst the luxuriant wisteria. J. M. Brydone started the solicitors' business when he lost his post as Lord Leconfield's land agent, having seriously exceeded his specification for the construction of Egremont Row. For all that however he remained on the friendliest terms with the great house. The firm would become at the turn of the century Brydone and Pitfield, then Pitfield and Oglethorpe, Oglethorpe and Anderson and now Anderson, Longmore and Higham.

Among the Petworth House Archives there is extant an account of a scene at a fair in Petworth in May 1734. The house was at that time a copyhold property "once Platts" and occupied by one Joseph Whicher an apothecary, quite likely that same Mr. Whicher of the 1762 Window Tax return. The house had at that time an awning at the front supported by five posts and forming a rough shed under which several people could operate stalls on fair and market days. Richard Smart, the clerk of the market, demanded from Mrs. Whitcombe, one of the stall-holders, sixpence for her standing. She refused, saying that she had already paid her show-penny for exposing goods for sale and that, as one of Mr. Whicher's tenants, she was not liable in respect of the Market Square itself. When, on Smart's behalf, Thomas Boxall the tithingman confiscated some tape from the stall in lieu of payment James Whicher appeared from the house and berated Smart for harassing his tenant. A fracas ensued and Joseph Whicher assaulted both Smart and Boxall.

The Duke of Somerset for whom Smart had been acting ordered an enquiry into the incident but James Whicher stood his ground, albeit apologising for his brother's assault. To substantiate his case Smart quoted one widow Lawnder of Lurgashall, whose father had formerly been clerk of the Market, as saying that her father had received an acknowledgement for the awning although she could not remember how much it had been. This was somewhat inconclusive as Gammer Lawnder, when questioned in turn by Joseph Whicher, denied saying anything of the kind and added that if Smart had reported her as saying anything of the kind he was a rascal. The awning at Platts had never been subject to such payment although the neighbouring White Hart (Austens), Roundabouts and Sandham's House (Avenings) had made some such payments.

Betty Bevis (*Petworth Society Bulletin* No. 23) remembers the periodic visits of the "picture show" just after the 1914-1918 war. The exhibitors, itinerants with portable equipment, would set up in the open air as soon as it was dark enough. "The screen would be put up over the window at the left-hand side of the main entrance to the Solicitors' office . . . and a large crowd would soon gather."

The ancient site that is now Austens the ironmongers was already Thomas Vyvyan's Belchambers in John Ederton's 1541 return, but by the seventeenth century had become an inn, the White Hart, often called the Great White Hart to distinguish it from its satellite beerhouse the Little White Hart on the corner of Trump Alley. For a while it was the premier inn in Petworth and the survival of detailed inventories from 1670 and 1758 enabled Hugh Kenyon (*Petworth Town and Trades* pp. 122f) to offer a tentative analysis of the fortunes of the inn over the period between the two inventories.

In 1670 under Henry Goble the inn had a number of painted chambers, among them the Cock, the Falcon, the Griffin, the Dolphin, the Hart, the Luce, the Angel, the Star, the Marigold and the Sun. Luce is an old word for a pike. These rooms, mostly bed-chambers on the first floor, would have been elaborately decorated with appropriate murals. All but the Angel, Griffin, Hart and Marigold had disappeared by the time of the later inventory and this may be attributed partly to changing fashions and an increased use of prints and pictures, but partly too to the White Hart having lost ground to its great rival the Half Moon just across the Market Square. Thomas Watts succeeded Jane Johnson in 1758 but by the time of James Crow's survey of 1779, the inn had become a private house occupied by Thomas Woodyer. When it was sold in 1789 it was already described as "formerly the White Hart Inn" (Beck, *Inns* p. 139).

The ironmongery business dates from the early nineteenth century. Indeed Mr. Greenfield (or more probably his annotator) will have it that Mr. Row, the founder of the business had his first ironmonger's shop at Daintrey House in East Street. Whatever the truth of this, the Market Square premises had been an ironmongers for a good fifty years before its purchase by B. S. Austen in 1866. It appears to have been Austen who had the old inn building demolished to make way for entirely new premises. It is fortunate that William Knight made accurate drawings of the old inn building prior to demolition in 1866. The drawings seem to have been made with the specific purpose of accompanying an article by Roger Turner in SAC xix, an article which has been much castigated over the years for its erroneous claim that the inn premises had been the site of the Great George rather than the Great White Hart. This manifest error does not completely invalidate the article however, still less William Knight's drawings. Turner is accurate enough when he writes of the old inn as being "in its architectural form like the letter H. That is, it consisted of an eastern and western wing, the western fronting to the Market Place and the two being connected by a somewhat narrower building consisting principally of a passage and staircase and carried at right angles from one to another about midway."

William Knight's original drawings from July 1866 have been lost for years but have surfaced recently and quite unexpectedly in a Surrey attic. They are reproduced here by courtesy of Mr. and Mrs. Waldy. They are much clearer than the etchings made from them for the SAC article. Drawing No. 1 shows the brick and stucco front as it was in 1866, accurately described a few years previously as "a long low house opposite the Market Clock" (*Petworth Society Bulletin* No. 31). Drawing No. 2 shows the original frontage which had been almost entirely obscured by the brick facing. Drawing No. 3 shows the courtyard, for such it effectively was, with the dotted lines over the doorways indicating the passage and stairs that formed the link between the two wings. A fourth drawing (not reproduced) shows the rear of the premises.

In April 1866 the whole premises, late Seward's and formerly Row's, were to let at a rent of £60 per annum or at a commuted rent of £50 "without the rooms used now by the 'Albert Institute'." Alternatively the entire premises might be purchased for the sum of £825. (Letter from Death and Son to B. S. Austen 11/4/66 Courtesy

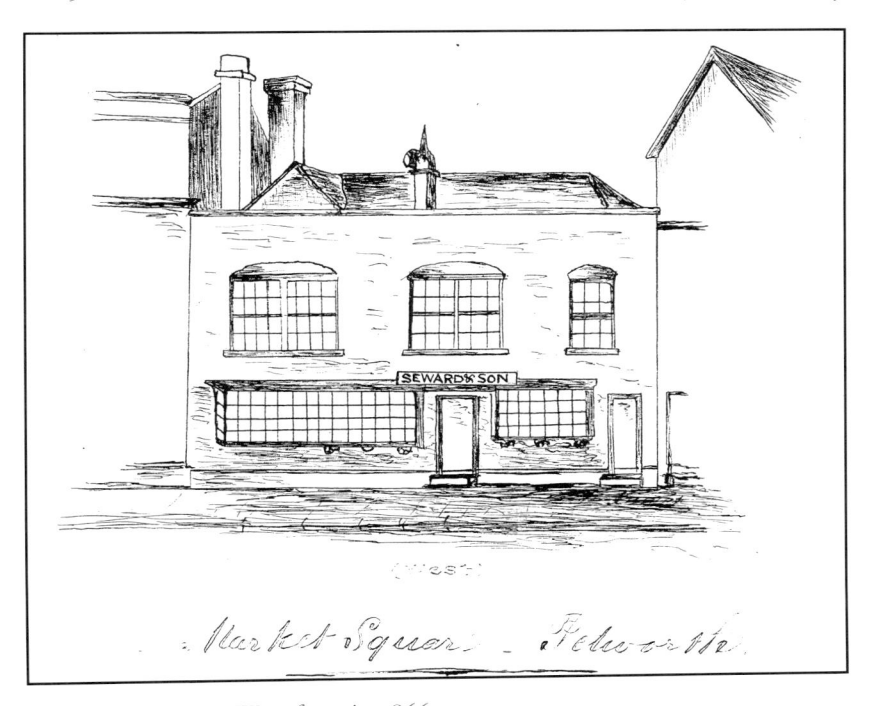

DRAWING NO. 1 The West front in 1866

TREAD LIGHTLY HERE

*As Built-A.D. 1663.*

DRAWING NO. 2 The West front with the facade removed. Note the small room with gable roof over the south entrance passage.

DRAWING NO. 3 The inner or eastern part of the building after the removal of the west wing. The dotted lines show the position of the connecting passage and stairs.

of Mr. Philip Neve.) The Albert Institute was the foundation of Thomas Seward, later to be prominent at the East Street Institute. He clearly had no desire to follow the family tradition of ironmongery.

The appearance of B. S. Austen and the demolition of what had once been the Great White Hart heralds the modern era. It is surely of B. S. Austen that Arch Newman wrote in the West Sussex Gazette of 22nd August 1968, "Then there was the tall hard-hatted and frock-coated ironmonger: he would walk outside his shop always ready to tell any casual person: "The man on the far side of the street owes me a lot of money". History recalls B. S. Austen perhaps as rather more discreet than that but Arch Newman, looking back over three score years or more, can perhaps be allowed a certain licence!

The property to the south of Austens has, at least on the face of it, a rather less accessible history. It is marked on the 1882 Estate Survey map as Allens or Lanes, the italic capitals indicating archaic names. Neither title bears obvious connection with known history and, indeed, the two names may simply be variants of a common original. Now a pet shop, the premises were for generations "Pelletts", confectioners, tobacconists and hairdressers. Petworth Post Office occupied these premises in the nineteenth century, only moving from Market Square when the East Street office was built in the second decade of this century. The postmaster in 1826 was John Easton and Pigot's Directory for that year announces that the "Mail from London arrives every morning at four and is despatched at ten at night; from Chichester and Arundel at nine at night and returns at five in the morning". A long day it would seem. By 1853 Kelly's Directory has the redoubtable George Arnold "organist, prof. of music, postmaster, Master of Charity School and Vestry Clerk" in charge. One wonders how one man managed to reconcile such varied and exacting duties. Arnold clearly did and did so for many years.

Next to Allens or Lanes lay in older times Durance, long the family mansion of the Barnard family and mentioned by John Ederton in 1541 as in the occupation of Henry Ubley. Durance was a large house and inventories survive for Thomas Barnard (1666) and Henry Barnard (1697) both described as "gentlemen". The

TREAD LIGHTLY HERE

Old Petworth Post Office. Market Square about 1880. *Photograph by Walter Kevis. Garland Collection.*

inventories give an extensive range of rooms, even, in 1666, mentioning a banqueting house. This was, as Kenyon suggests, (p. 105) "probably detached and possibly used for concerts and dances". Some Barnard household accounts are extant in PHA but are not in fact particularly informative. They date from the late seventeenth century. The Barnard family had probably made their money as tallow chandlers, John Barnard Junior's inventory of 1681 indicates this clearly enough (Kenyon p. 112) and later generations lived off the wealth accrued in trade. The lack of any impetus to work led in the fullness of time to the family house being heavily mortgaged and in the 1740s to Thomas Barnard being imprisoned for debt (Kenyon p. 57). Durance was purchased by the Third Earl of Egremont in 1800: part of the premises being pulled down to make the present junction with New Street, part either renovated or rebuilt as the present chemist's shop. The new shop would in its turn be conveyed to Mr. Johnson the tailor in exchange for his house "Roundabouts", free-standing in the Market Square and pulled down to facilitate the movement of traffic from New Street (PHA deeds OH 10 AA). John Greenfield specifically mentions Tailor Johnson's house as the Roundabouts (*Tales* p. 93) and Arnold's *History* (p. 89) says that the term came "from its Rotundo-like appearance". Neither Greenfield nor Arnold would in fact have seen the building but there would certainly be recollection of it in the Arnold family. Charles F. Johnson appears in the 1851 census as a draper and chemist, carrying on the same dual business that William Johnson had done before him. Pigot's 1826 Directory gives William Johnson as a "linen draper and druggist". Alfred Holt is described in the 1871 census however simply as a draper. It was to this shop that George Steggles would move at the turn of the century from his premises in the churchyard and for the next three decades make very much his own. George Steggles worked long hours and never took a holiday in his life. His skill in dispensing was legendary: not for nothing was he popularly known as "Doc" Steggles. Dispensing was by no means the whole business; illogically perhaps to modern ways of thinking, chemists in older days tended also to be purveyors of cigarettes. Greta Steggles (*Petworth Society Bulletin* No. 58) remembers two particular brands: Evening Star and Players No. 2 as being in demand . . .

"My father bought them in boxes containing two hundred or more cigarettes and, for sale, they were packed into bundles wrapped in small squares of white paper, sealed with sealing wax. Evening Star sold at fifteen cigarettes for seven pence and Players Number 2, a slightly better quality, at fourteen for seven pence halfpenny."

Confectionery too, if of a rather specialised kind was another staple item of stock . . .

"My father was very fond of children and those that came into the shop were frequently given a sweet — a large strong acid drop or a blackcurrant pastille — from the big jars which, with other medicinal tablets stood behind the counter, and the really lucky ones would be given a block of Allen & Hanbury's, or Ovaltine, chocolate. Elizabeth Wyndham, the adopted daughter of Lord and Lady Leconfield often came into the shop with her nanny and, when she had her first Shetland pony insisted upon bringing it up the two steps and right into the shop "to show Mr. Steggles".

George Steggles' shop window functioned as something of an unofficial parish notice-board . . .

"I don't think that I ever remember seeing the things in the windows of the shop changed. Apart from a row of carboys on a shelf at the top, the New Street window was always filled with animal medicines and other farming requirements. Cooper's Sheep Dip is one that comes to my mind. It really did not matter what was in the window facing the Square for it was always so full of posters announcing whist drives, dances and other functions that nothing else could be seen. It was recognised as the place in the town for displaying notices and I can remember that Mr. Stevenson, the Boys' school headmaster, (long before the days of radio or T.V.) when in most years he attended the Oxford and Cambridge Boat race, sent telegrams to my father, announcing the result, which were then put into the window for all to see."

The present estate agents on the south-east side of the Square is traditionally a butcher's shop and may be the former copyhold shop in the Market purchased by the Earl of Egremont in 1802 and rebuilt as a butcher's shop with a bedroom over it "for one

Reading". (PHA deeds OG 13/39). The original deed would need to be consulted to confirm this. Arnold writing in 1864 reckoned that bull-baiting had not been extinct in Petworth more than sixty years when he gave the lectures on which his *History* is based, so it may well be at this very window that a candle burned to indicate that the flesh of the tortured animal was now for sale. Arnold had been told by an old inhabitant that at least once the bull had broken loose from its tormentors and charged the ring "to the no small disconcertment of the surrounding throng". (Arnold p. 90.) A masterly understatement one would think. The shop was still a butcher's as the century turned, Moyers for many years, then later Motts. A photograph from the early 1890s shows one Stanford as proprietor. George Peacock recalls being employed by Mr. Moyer in the early 1920s, working from seven in the morning to six at night to learn the trade and run errands, delivering the meat on the old-fashioned shallow, oblong, wooden trays that were carried over the shoulder. There was a regular weekly round to Graffham and the errand boy might be sent out on his bike with any extras or omissions. The main delivery would be by cob-cart. The slaughter-house was in Trump Alley and the quarters of beef would be carried (or wheeled) down New Street to the Market Square shop.

The errand boy also biked out three times a week to deliver to Duncton, finishing his round at the top of Duncton High Street. This would be in the morning and in the afternoon he would cut up meat for sausages. Often too he would make the long walk to Petworth Station to take the train to Pulborough. He would wait until the market finished, then with a representative from each of the other two Petworth butchers, Mr. Payne and Mr. Boorer, drive the animals, pigs, sheep or oxen, back through Fittleworth and Hesworth to Petworth. George Peacock recalled Mr. Duval as manager in his time and knives being ground on a whetstone. As the boy turned the handle Mr. Moyer would stand with the knife. He recalled too ice being delivered by Colbrooks of Guildford.

The Star is a very old-established inn but not under its present name, nor, probably in its present form. The premises appear to have been rebuilt in the eighteenth century. If this is indeed the inn referred to as the Black Bull the premises had been leased by one William Heath from the Earl of Northumberland in 1591 (Beck,

*Inns* p. 141). In the eighteenth century the inn came into the possession of John Edsaw a distiller who also owned the large southerly adjoining house called Mansers. The two properties would henceforth always go together as "the Bull Inn and Mansers". A new owner, Edward Puttock changed the name at the close of the eighteenth century. Certainly by the time of an auction sale of the stock in trade of Thomas Edwards in December 1813 (WSRO SP 88) the house is clearly and unequivocally the Star. The "four-post", bureau and press Bedsteds, with check furniture; seven feather beds; Blankets and Quilts" suggest that travellers found the Star a more than useful staging post.

In the early years of the present century Henry Whitcomb could recall Master Collins, then the licensee, keeping his chicken in the stabling at the side of the pub. Every morning he would let his chicken out to scratch about under the carts. The stabling at the side is shown in very old photographs as a house, occupied for a long period in the nineteenth century by William Stoper Wright the coppersmith and brazier. Wright also owned the adjoining butchers shop for a time although he appears to have operated his tinsmith's business from home.

West of the Star is the important site occupied at present by Gateway but formerly the International Stores, who had moved down from New Street in the mid-1920s. Mr. Davidson had had the premises for a while after the Great War but from Victorian times they had been Otways the grocers, once Otway and Fuller. The 1851 census has another grocer here, Edward Holt, described in Kelly's Directory of 1853 as "grocer and tallow chandler". How long the premises had been used as a grocer's prior to Holt's time is not clear. The 1882 survey map calls the site "the Dyehouse", the italic capitals as usual on the map indicating an archaic name. Whether this takes the dyehouse back to Petworth's sixteenth century cloth-making heyday is at present impossible to say but it would certainly seem not unlikely. In the 1690s Lord Leconfield (*Petworth Manor* p. 117) knows of one Joseph Morris apothecary, who, "it seems, conducted his profession at the Dyehouse near the Market Place". Unfortunately Leconfield gives no documentation for this. Clearly by this time the dyehouse as such was no more: Morris would seem to have had shop premises of some kind with a

## MARKET SQUARE

The west side of Market Square in May 1928. Messrs. Cockshutt centre, the Bus Office on the left. *Photograph by George Garland. Garland Collection.*

house and garden. In 1658 the Dyehouse had been the property of Thomas Levett, while in 1656 John Drew had been presented before the manorial court for throwing dye water into the gutter in Market Place. As the offence does not occur again Leconfield not unreasonably concludes that the dyehouse had ceased to operate by the late seventeenth century. William Warren the clothworker from Heath End has a dyehouse mentioned in his inventory and is known to have had a fulling-mill, but he seems to have been based at Coultershaw and Heath End farm. He died in 1711. Petworth may have had several dyehouses at different times. The open drain would carry the waste water from the Market Place Dyehouse over Damer's Bridge and away. Of the one hundred and fifty years between Joseph Morris the apothecary and Edward Holt the grocer we have at present no information.

Nora Hollingdale recalls working at the International Stores in the early 1930s (*Petworth Society Bulletin* No. 41) . . .

"When I left the International Stores in 1935 it was still conducted very much on the old-fashioned principle of being served by the assistants, as opposed to present-day ideas of serving yourself. You would say what you wanted and the assistants would get it for you. The centre space was basically left vacant with the fixtures and shelving hugging the walls. The counters ran round the perimeter. As you went in there was a long counter to your left for bacon, cheese and fats, while another counter catered for jams, marmalades, teas and biscuits. There was a counter just for fruit and I can remember bananas at a penny halfpenny each. On the right hand side as you entered were the patent medicines, sweets and sugar. Just inside the door on the right was the cash desk where Edna Nairn and Miss Rapley would sit. There was at that time a door in the corner so that effectively the cash desk controlled the two exits.

There was a great deal of manual work to be done and the International then carried a staff of some sixteen to eighteen, including a number of men. There was a delivery service and Mr. Field was employed to go round taking people's orders. As I have said, the store operated as did all others in those days, on the principle that you would indicate what you wanted and it would be cut or picked out for you by the assistants. Bacon might be rashered in a variety of different thicknesses and would be cut as you waited.

The cheeses were of the old-fashioned kind, needing to be skinned before cutting. Butter was still done in pats. A customer would order a pound of Sylvan Glen for 1/2d. and it would be cut straight from the block. It was rather similar with sweets: they would be on the shelves in boxes and jars and weighed out for you as you wanted them, at eight pence a pound. Christmas was a particularly busy time because people would begin from about mid-November to take out their clubs. They'd start in January, paying in at the desk at a rate of so much a week, a shilling perhaps. This would be marked down on a special card, separate from the weekly account. At Christmas time the club orders would come in like a flood: people wanted things like dried fruit and peel for Christmas puddings or glacé cherries and sultanas for cakes. We might have to work till 10 o'clock to get the club orders finished but there would be no extra money for the time we had spent.

Every week two of the staff had to go out the back and down the steps into the warehouse. Here they used to weigh up the different sugars, flour, rolled oats, soda, all sorts of things which were weighed up out of great bins and bagged up in small quantities to be ready when the customers wanted them. Items like flour were bagged up in 1½ lbs. 3 lbs. and 6 lbs. units and stacked up in great piles ready for the counters. The sugars too, granulated, moist, caster, lump and preserving, also needed to be bagged up.

Each counter tended to be a unit on its own and individual staff would be responsible for filling up before they went home. As you served a customer, you gave them a numbered white ticket, wrote the price on the ticket and initialled it. The cashiers had spikes and as the tickets were brought to the cash desk to be paid, the numbered tickets would be stuck down on the spike. If a number was missing they would know that particular ticket hadn't been settled, and they would call out, say, number seventeen, to check. Customers would tend to pay after a visit to a particular counter, then go to another counter, collect another ticket, pay, and move to another counter. It was almost like a series of different shops under one roof. It did take a while longer than modern shopping but of course one counter might have several different items, i.e. bacon, cheese and butter would all go together and come on the same ticket.

Fixtures were mainly attached to the walls and the customer would look to the outside of the containers and order from the shelf.

Sometimes the prices were printed on the box or jar but often we just had to remember. Biscuits were another item for the customer to point to and for us to weight out. For weighing we had the old-fashioned scales with brass weights."

This account of Otways appeared in the *West Sussex Times and Sussex Standard* for 4th February 1893 . . .

West Sussex Industries.

NO. 7 MESSRS. OTWAY AND FULLERS, PETWORTH.

There may even yet be people who think that to be a grocer is only to stand behind a counter all day, and wile away the hours in such pleasing occupations as sweeping money into the till, or in sampling currants and raisins. That might or might not — probably not — have been the experience of grocers a dozen or so years back, but it is very different now. The business man has to work hard, and if he is to retain, much less build up a connection, he must zealously study the tastes of his customers, and must be always ready to cater to their liking.

In West Sussex there is a firm, that of Messrs. Otway and Fuller, which, from a very small beginning, has by sheer force of merit and good management pushed its way into the very foremost place. In August, 1858 — 35 years ago — Mr. George Otway founded the house. As we have already said, the beginning was not a very big one, but it was sound, and soundness is worth much more than a lot of flashy shams. From the very first Mr. Otway saw that in order to build up a big business he would have to go outside Petworth. Then the town was considerably more prosperous than at present, on account of the county business transacted there. Still, Mr. Otway foresaw it would not be big enough for him. The shop in Market-square, which is still one of the firm's houses, had been tenantless for two years prior to 1858. It had been used as a grocery and tallow chandlery. In re-opening it Mr. Otway wisely decided to let the candle business alone, except so far as retailing these useful commodities in the ordinary way of business was concerned. Resolving not to spend his time behind the counter waiting for customers, Mr. Otway, full of energy as he was, went out to look for trade. He was successful from the first. People like to be spared all

MARKET SQUARE

Otways about 1890. *Photograph by Walter Kevis. Garland Collection.*

the trouble they can, and this Mr. Otway found. They gave him their orders, and the goods were punctually delivered. During the first week of his trading career, the humble donkey cart was found to be capable of going the rounds. The week after, however, Mr. Otway found a stronger animal was necessary. He arranged for the part-ownership of a pony, but in a very short time his punctuality and his integrity in business were so far recognised that he had to acquire the pony for his sole use. The next step was to have a good sized cart built, and this, in its turn, had to give way to a van. These doings years ago, cannot be compared with the business the firm is now carrying on. Eight large pair-horsed vans are now required to cope with the family trade in the district, and every week one huge van is loaded up till three horses have a fairly hard task to draw it.

Mr. George Otway retired from the business in July, 1886, and was succeeded by his son, Mr. F. G. Otway. The establishment had by this time grown to such an extent as to be almost too big for one man to control. A year later therefore Mr. Otway took Mr. Fuller into partnership, and the firm attained its present style of Otway and Fuller. At the commencement of the partnership the extensive premises in Golden-square were acquired, and the handsomely-furnished shop, which is far ahead of anything else in the neighbourhood as regards fittings and stock, was opened. The subsequent history of the firm has been much the same as that which preceded it — a record of continuous prosperity. And in spite of increasing competition there can be no doubt that as the business is conducted now it will go on increasing, for the public are not slow to appreciate the advantages of dealing at a really reliable and honourable house.

Petworth is extremely old-fashioned, so far as appearances go, but it is by no means behind the rest of the world. It is full of roomy, comfortable looking, solidly built, old-fashioned houses, and cosy shops, built for wear and not for cheapness. In Market-square, which is the centre of the quaint town, the most prominent business-house is that of Messrs. Otway and Fuller. From its very appearance one can tell that it is a shop where full value for money can be obtained. There is no puffed up trash, no flaring inducements to buy inferior goods at double their value. On the contrary the very aspect of the place — its neatness, perfect order, and cleanness, convince the customer that Messrs. Otway and Fuller can, as they do, confidently invite the public to "give things a test,

MARKET SQUARE

Mazawattee tea advertising material. Some have "Otway and Fuller" stamped on the back.

then choose the best." The stock here is extremely large, and it includes everything that can come under the head of groceries and provisions. Quite recently, too, the firm have added another branch, and they are now vendors of patent medicines. Very much cut up is this patent medicine business nowadays. The public take abundance of physic indeed, but they will have it cheap; therefore the man who is satisfied with the least profit does most business. Messrs. Otway and Fuller's prices are considerably below the "stores' lists." It is interesting to know which of the compounds under the protection of the Government stamp goes down best with the British public. In this connection Messrs. Otway and Fuller, who from the enormous business they transact may fairly claim to be experts in dispensing patent medicines, inform us that Beecham takes the lead, and is a long way ahead of anybody else.

Trading has in many respects been revolutionised since the days of our grandfathers, but in one respect at least old notions are still clung to. The modern grocer must keep good teas. Now, here is where the most difficult part of the business comes in, and where the local trader, if he knows his work, has the advantage over outsiders. It is a fact not so well known as it ought to be that the richness and flavour of a cup of tea depends very much on the water by the aid of which it has been brewed. Tea which proves fragrant and invigorating in one neighbourhood often turns out to be altogether insipid when brewed elsewhere. Knowing this full well, Messrs. Otway and Fuller have paid the greatest attention to the subject, and as a result they supply teas which are exactly suited to the water of the district. By purchasing from them consumers reap the advantage of the firm's study and experience. Judicious blending of teas is another point to which great care is devoted. At present, Chinese tea has almost entirely gone out of fashion, and it has been replaced by the products of India and Ceylon. The most popular Ceylon teas are those which are sold in packets. Messrs. Otway and Fuller do an enormous trade in this direction. They are agents for the well-known Mazawattee blend, and their rapid sales are a guarantee that customers receive the newest and freshest growths. What the grocer has to do is to so blend different teas as to make the one supplement the other, and to ensure a fragrant refreshing cup. In tea-blending Messrs. Otway and Fuller excel. Unlike many country houses, they do not have their teas in ready mixed, but the blending is carefully performed on their own premises, with the result that the firm have become noted for the excellence of their teas. Buying at the right time, and paying prompt cash, they are enabled to sell as low as anyone, and at the same time to give a better quality than many houses can afford. Coffee, too, receives great attention from the firm, so as to obtain the utmost flavour from the berry. Then the coffee is ground, and until it passes to the consumer it is kept in air-tight canisters.

As provision merchants Messrs. Otway and Fuller do an enormous business. They have a well-appointed sausage factory from which issue the celebrated Petworth sausages. So great is the demand for these delicacies that during the season hundreds of pounds go out every week. Large quantities are sent by post all over the country, and among other notable people the firm supply the Duke of Connaught. The manufacture is carried out under the supervision of one of the principals. The best-fed pigs in the district are bought by the firm. They are killed in the slaughterhouses at the rear of the Golden-square premises. Thence the meat, judiciously mixed with the proper seasonings, goes to the sausage-making room. Modern machinery driven by a gas engine minces the juicy meat to the utmost fineness at the rate of 15 pounds a minute, and a second piece of machinery does the filling and completes the work. The secret of the success achieved in this branch lies in the fact that the sausages are made entirely from the best meat, and that no bread whatever is used. In the majority of sausages a considerable percentage of bread will be found, because bread is cheaper than pork, but this is not the case with those of Messrs. Otway and Fuller's manufacture. Scrupulous attention is given to ensure absolute cleanliness, and directly after use the whole of the machinery is taken to pieces and thoroughly scoured. A large trade is also done in pork, besides which the firm cure bacon and hams. At the rear of the Market-square shop they have a large smoking house, which is nearly always full of hams and sides in process of smoking. Here again the personal supervision of the heads of the firm is given to the work, for from first to last — from the selection of the meat to determining when the operation of smoking shall cease — experience and skill are necessary to bring about complete success.

The best idea of the magnitude of the firm's business can be gained by a walk round their stores and warehouses. As this would be impracticable for most people, we will endeavour to give some slight description. Most of the stock is kept on the Golden-square premises, which are of very great extent. The sausage factory is there and, at the extreme end, the slaughter-house. The latter, as well as all the things used therein, are as clean as the proverbial new pin, and are kept sweet by frequent flushings and scourings. Coffee is ground in a room which adjoins that in which sausages are made. In another apartment hard by is machinery for grinding malt. Many Petworth people cling to the old-fashioned practice of brewing their own beer, consequently Messrs. Otway and Fuller have a large demand for malt and hops, which, like all their stock, is of the best quality.

Under the same roof is a very large cheese store. The extent of this may be imagined from the fact that the racks are capable of holding nearly 1,000 cheeses. A large number is always in stock, for as fast as cheeses ripen and are sold out new ones take their places. The stock includes Gorgonzolas, American, and the old-fashioned Dutch. Anxious as they always are to promote local enterprise, the firm once gave Sussex cheeses a trial. The experiment was not, however, a success. For some reason or other good cheese, it would appear, cannot be made in this county; at all events Messrs. Otway and Fuller were unable to procure any that could at all compete with the products of other districts.

Another cool, clean, and airy room is stocked with the finest New Zealand mutton, and the best American beef. This is a department of the firm's business which has been but recently undertaken. It has, however, proved eminently successful. The meat is received fresh every day, and is therefore always in prime condition, and it is sold at prices which no one can cavil at. Large underground stores, which are remarkably cool even in the heighth of summer, well ventilated, and perfectly free from damp, enable the firm to keep butter and other commodities such as aerated waters in splendid condition at all times. With regard to butter they guarantee that all they sell is absolutely pure and genuine. Here, again, the advantage of dealing with such a firm is at once apparent, since their extensive operations enable them to sell at lower prices than smaller traders find possible, even with an inferior article. Coming up again we get to the flour store. The firm have always a large quantity in stock. All their supplies are from mills in the neighbourhood, and consist exclusively of best English roller-ground flour. On the upper floor of the capacious store-houses are rooms full of Crosse & Blackwell's delicacies: jams; spices and flavourings from all climes; and in short, large quantities of all those goods which are sold by first-class grocers. One large room is entirely devoted to fruit, and here are boxes and boxes of selected raisins, currants, sultanas, &c. Then there is a room in which the tea-blending is carried on and another in which the leaded chests from India, China, and Ceylon, are stored. In the ground floor room are kept large supplies of salt, soda, soap, and a miscellany of articles suitable for keeping the homes of their customers bright and healthy. With regard to sugars, Messrs. Otway and Fuller make a point of always keeping a large stock of that produced from West Indian canes, as well as the now more common continental beet sugar.

The firm has always had a good name for liberally treating those in its employ, now numbering nearly thirty. This is particularly applicable with regard to the young men engaged by the firm. Messrs. Otway and Fuller keep a large and comfortable house near the shop for them, and take great care to render it as homelike as possible. The training that these young men undergo at Petworth is thoroughly sound. It has stood many of them in good stead, for several who were once assistants to Mr. Otway or the present firm, have now, thanks in a great measure to their old employers, first-rate businesses of their own, or hold responsible positions as managers or travellers.

That the firm has attained to so conspicuous a position, and one which it not only keeps but steadily improves, is due primarily to the fact that its founder was always very careful that everything connected with the business should be done straightforwardly and uprightly, and that he — as his successors do now — always maintained the strictest integrity. People used to say — and no doubt there are some who say so now — that a grocer could not be honest and yet prosperous. But Mr. Otway lived to prove the contrary. His aim was to get a fair profit out of everything. That was easily done in those days, but now no grocer has conscientious scruples because he is making too great gain. The difficulty often is to get any margin of profit at all. During the first year that Mr. Otway, senior, traded he gained nothing. But, on the other hand, he did not lose, and he had made the ground firm for subsequent success. During the second year things began to move, and he was able to begin the practice, which he never discontinued, of laying by a set sum for charitable purposes. He experienced, too, that the satisfaction that comes from giving is greater than that which is occasioned by receiving. The traditions established by him are worthily maintained by his successors. They may with pride point to the fact that the firm is still going ahead, and to the fact that they have solved the great problem — where to get the best quality articles at the lowest prices.

It is difficult to say whether the Swan premises on the west side of the Market Square should be included in Saddlers Row or Market Square. Certainly they form an integral part of the west side of the Square but they form also far the greater part of the northern side of Saddlers Row. The old Swan (demolished in 1899) fronted unequivocally on to the Market Square while the new Swan had its imposing front on Saddlers Row. E. V. Lucas was less than impressed with the new building, "it might," he testily averred, "be at Balham". (*Highways and Byways* 1904 p. 103). The old Swan was an important inn and the premises are referred to as we have seen as early as John Ederton's 1541 return as "Serles, once Agnes Berkfords," a title that would endure over the centuries. The 1541 reference is earlier than the earliest surviving title deed known to Miss Beck which comes from 1587 (Beck, p. 137). A first explicit reference to the "sign of the Swan" comes from a conveyance of 1606 (Beck, ibid.). The following entry in the Barnard accounts (PHA 6354) is "for a pound of tobacco att the Swann this 25 ffebr. [16]80"

The old building, while smaller than the new, occupied the same ground and was provided with numerous outhouses including a dissenting chapel, probably a predecessor of the Providence Chapel in Golden Square, Benjamin Challen, benefactor of the Golden Square chapel selling the inn to the Leconfield Estate in 1840 for £2100 (Beck, p. 138).

It was to this west side of the Market Square that the station bus would bring its passengers. The Swan was, as Kelly's Directory for 1853 says "a posting-house". Photographs survive of the bus pulling up outside the old inn in the time of Mr. Pyecroft the last incumbent. Previous to him Charles Dempster had kept the inn for many years. The massive slate sign of the old Swan is still at Petworth House.

The 1882 Survey map does not offer an archaic name for the old Bank House premises to the north of the Swan Inn, marking them simply as "Bank". In default of an old name it is difficult to say whether or not the site is featured on John Ederton's 1541 return. The building has been divided during this century, the southern being a private house, the northern housing the offices of the Southdown Bus Co. Up until recent years the old Bank vaults survived. The usage of the building today is commercial and the two-fold division has continued. Victorian photographs of the exterior show the bank as occupying the entire ground floor to the front at least. The premises were exchanged with Leconfield in 1900, the London and County Bank taking over the Half Moon site across the road and the Leconfield Estate the former Bank House (PHA deeds 14/8/1-25). PHA deeds OH10/A120 indicate that there were originally two freehold houses on the site, the present house being either a new building or possibly a rebuilding of the two old houses. The latter possibility is suggested by Mr. R. Pottington's discovery of a small cache of documents during restoration work a few years ago. The dockets, for such they are, relate to the leatherworking business of Robert Willard and cover a period roughly from 1769 to 1781. They are mainly suppliers' bills for skins, as often as not from William Lewis of Midhurst. Grain skins are rough with a pimpled surface but the meaning of "wex" skins is not clear. Another bill is for men's and women's lasts, while one from Henry Eade is for a 42 lb hide at 1/1d a pound. An account of William Upton from 1781 reflects extensive alterations and mentions a lower window, the shop window and the cutting room window. This bill and the very survival of the dockets at all suggests that the new building may well have incorporated elements of the old. It would appear that Robert Willard would collect at least some of his skins himself. Reconciling an account William Lewis writes, "I did not reckon the skins right when you wass here".

By 1812 the house was the residence of Mr. Garland the tailor and scene of the most famous meal in Petworth's history, the Christmas week dinner party that Master Greenfield attended as a boy of ten (*Tales* pp. 11ff). Mr. Greenfield's inimitable account needs no repetition here. We may echo his disappointment with the thin soup but rejoice with him as the dinner really gets under way with the roasted fowls, large ham, potatoes and blue and white basin with about a quart of rich melted butter with chopped parsley in it. The characters Mr. Greenfield encountered need to be brought to life in his own pages rather than in these. We will simply leave our old friend and his family to plod their way home, with clogs and pattens, candles and lanthorns, "through the snow, ankle-deep" (*Tales* p. 28).

Mr. Greenfield (*Tales* p. 92) is clear enough about the dinner being in the parlour of the house "now the London and County Bank". He attributes the founding of the bank to Mr. William Upton, the next banker being William Stoveld. It was, he says, Mr. Upton who built the present front of the Bank House. One wonders if this is a distant, oral recollection of the alterations of 1781 or another completely separate renovation. Pigot's 1826 Directory lists under Bankers "Stovald, William and John. Draw on Masterman and Co. London." The cheque illustrated from the 1840s shows the bank as still a very personal affair, the cheques being drawn on Mr. Stovald himself. The spelling Stovald and Stoveld varies.

Bill Vincent vividly recalls the Bus Office in the 1920s (*Petworth Society Magazine* No. 59).

"When I was nine or ten I didn't have a part-time job but I had a friend who did and I would go round with him. He delivered evening papers. We'd go up to the Bus Office in Market Square — it was as much a waiting-room as an office in those days — to wait for the papers to come in. They'd be brought up on the bus that met every train. By this time Mr. Morais at the garage up the road had taken over the Bus Office. There was no Southdown then of course, but Henry Streeter, who had run the horse-bus for years, was still about. When we arrived he was usually sitting by the fire, twiddling his thumbs in the way that he did, half-asleep. I expect he was waiting for the next bus to take him back to Coultershaw where he kept the Railway Inn. By this time there was a Crossley ex-ambulance doing the run from the station but Charlie Mullins sometimes still took the horse and cab. Mr. Henley or occasionally Mr. Morais would drive the Crossley.

When the papers were in Mr. Weaver would come across from the shop and cut the bundles open, counting out so many for each boy."

One last important property on the west side is what was until recently the old Square Tavern, now diversified into an art gallery and a restaurant. Mr. F. R. "Fred" Knight operated as a baker here for years and before him Cockshutts, the baking tradition goes back well into the nineteenth century. An agreement between the trustees of the London and County Bank and Thomas Otway, baker, to sell the latter a passage running between their two properties apparently takes the bakery at least back to 1849.

An earlier agreement of 1786 however certainly antecedes the bakers. According to this, Henry Hind wishing to quit his business as a cooper, is prepared for a sum of £105 to make over his business to William Knight and to let "all those two shops, outhouse, shed and flight" [of stairs?] adjoining to and part of the premises now in Hind's occupation. Hind in his turn would retain the dwellinghouse with William Knight having first refusal to rent if Hind wishes to leave, or to buy if Hind should die before him. Each week Knight would supply Hind with two bushel baskets full of chips and assist him in bringing two tubs of water from either of the town's two conduits (documents copied from originals loaned by Mr. F. R. Knight). A William Knight is mentioned as a cooper in Pigot's 1826 Directory some forty years later.

An old name for the property seems to have been Hardhams, once embossed over the former entrance door to the south. It is just possible that this name goes back as far as John Ederton's return for he writes of "a tenement and garden and certain lands belonging to it called Hardhams" without specifying the location. It is possible too that the name is connected with Alexander Hardham, amerced by the manorial court in 1605 and 1606 for vagrant pigs and in 1606 for making a slaughter-house in his yard in the Market. (Leconfield, *Petworth Manor* pp. 128-129.) More likely the name is unconnected with either!

The area to the north has left little mark on history, at least on the face of it. The Red Cross Rooms were at one time the headquarters of the local Fire Brigade, then for a time public toilets, while the premises to the north were originally the Swan Livery Stables, then as the car gained in popularity, garage premises, for many years Harwoods.

This has been by some way the longest of these chapters and, in closing, I am conscious not only that I have had to omit a good deal but also that the Market Square, far more than the other Petworth streets, is greater than the sum of its parts. It is here that an older Petworth would come together, in the days when radio and television were unknown, to celebrate national events, Queen Victoria's Diamond Jubilee perhaps or King Edward VII's Coronation, a tradition continued in later years with the festivities and thanksgiving for V.E. Day in 1945. A newer Petworth too will on high occasions still come together in Market Square. Who can forget the triumphant return of the Toronto Scottish Regiment in 1985, the Canadians with their blazers and glengarries tumbling out of their coaches to meet a tumultuous welcome? Petworth Square is the ancestral home of Petworth's immemorial fair, the stalls and machines appearing almost like a dream on the 19th November to disappear again by midnight on the 20th as if they had never been. The Market Square and Petworth itself need such rare occasions to assert themselves against the traffic that on more ordinary days threatens to throttle it and destroy its spirit.

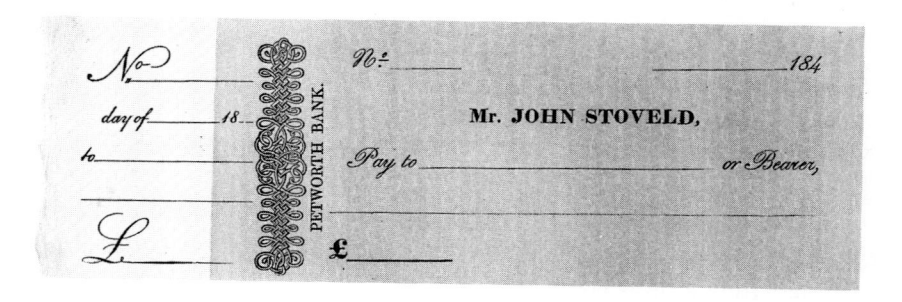

An 1840s cheque from Stoveld's bank.

The Iron Room in Market Square. 23rd July 1963. *Photograph by George Garland. Garland Collection.*

TREAD LIGHTLY HERE

Messrs. Ayling. Saddlers Row 1880s.

## 14

## SADDLERS ROW

SADDLERS Row is another essential arm of the town's one-way system; all southbound traffic being channelled through this narrow passageway. Except for the shoe-shop on the corner, the Swan Inn has always dominated the northern side of the street. Fragmented now, the former inn premises still appear to an extent as a cohesive whole. The north side of the street would have been cheerless enough when the old Swan Inn kept still its decaying outbuildings and malthouse. Edwin Saunders recalls . . .

> "Now I get to Saddlers Row and there was a large brewery. The man's name was Mr. Pyecroft and he was noted for his beer. He used to supply a good many public houses and used to go a good many miles with his beer. He brewed beer in my time — I have seen the maltster turning the corn, getting it ready to be brewed and I have seen the steam coming from the coppers. The man's name was Mr. Puddick and he was the last man to brew the beer: it was all done away with. Mr. Pyecroft was also noted for his fine horses; he used to have a beautiful pair of grey horses and the vans were always well looked-after."

When the old Swan was demolished at the turn of the century the new building had its front facing on to Saddlers Row. The entrance of course still remains. Those who lived opposite, might, in days when ease of travel was less to be taken for granted than now, glimpse the famous coming down those steps. Who more so in Goodwood week than Steve Donohue the jockey?

The name Saddlers Row, or Sadlers Row as it is often spelt, is not particularly old. The 1841 and 1851 census returns simply refer to Pound Street, Saddlers Row as such occurring first in the 1861 returns. The name will almost certainly be connected with the long-lived saddlers shop on the southern side. William Barttellot was there in 1841 and 1851 and Henry Ayling had moved down

201

there from High Street by 1861 and was still in occupation in 1881. The last saddler would be James Weeks. By the 1920s the shop had become Harpers, tobacconists, confectioners and hairdressers and is now Baskerville Antiques. Pym Harper also ran a taxi service for many years. The beginnings of the saddler's shop are unchronicled but Richard Barttellot, mentioned in Pigot's 1826 Directory as specialising in whip and coach harness, and again in the 1851 census as a retired saddler living at the shop with his son, may reasonably be conjectured to have been at this site in 1826. It is likely too that it is the Barttellot family and their long connection with this site to which the street owes its name.

Traditional as was the saddler's shop, the corner premises were just as traditionally a baker's. Ann Lane, widow, had the premises in 1851 and we may surmise that the James Lane mentioned as a baker by Pigot in 1826 had perhaps been at the Swan Corner even then. At any rate, the baking connection, if in varying hands, would continue for many years. The bakers and saddlers were, and are, structurally closely connected and appear in the 1882 Survey Map under a single name "Stringers". The italic writing as usual indicates an archaic name. While the 1882 map is to be treated with the greatest respect, the name Stringers is not to be found in extant deeds (cf WSRO MP 2573) and remains something of a mystery. John Ederton may make mention of the property in his 1541 return but, in the absence of an archaic name other than Stringers to provide identification, it is difficult to be sure. Ederton places "Serles, once Agnes Berkfords" in Market Place but could he go further and treat the south side of Saddlers Row as Market Place too? It appears doubtful. A clue may be provided by his reference to "John Polyng for a cottage near the forge and near Sowters Dyche once Thomas Shepherd's". There is no doubt that there was a forge on the south-east corner of Saddlers Row from at least 1670 and it is just possible that it was the same forge mentioned by Ederton in 1541. Sowter Dyche is at any rate the old name for Damer's Bridge.

Treswell's 1610 map shows a large building extending westward on the south side of the street and certainly encompassing the two properties on the east. They appear to have formed part of a sprawling larger premsies known in earlier times as the Bullhouse. A conveyance of 1666 from Algernon 10th Earl of Northumberland to Henry Barwick (PHA deeds OD2/C2) referring to the Bull may deal with this property rather than the Black Bull Inn in the Market Square. Whether the two Bulls are connected, and they are it has to be said very close together, is uncertain. An old name for the corner is Bull Corner, as later of course it would be Swan Corner. The original Bullhouse buildings may to an extent have been renovated by the 10th Earl prior to 1666 (WSRO MP 2573). Thomas Williams and George Lucas were tenants at this time and Lucas is known to have been a locksmith. His inventory (Kenyon p. 89) clearly indicates a forge of some kind on the site. Lucas had one anvil, one beckhorn, three sledges, three hammers, four vices, 18 filters and other working tools, not to mention a pair of bellows, two grindstones and a hundredweight of iron. It is tempting to speculate that the forge had continued since John Ederton's time and before but we cannot be sure that either forge or position were identical. Lucas' inventory gives his house four chambers, a kitchen, a shop and a cellar. I am not sure what a "beckhorn" is.

The saddler's shop is very much connected with the Washington family in the late seventeenth and early eighteenth century as the stone, found in the roof and set now into the side of the shop door, still shows. John Washington had left the whole property to his sons when he died in 1684, it being then divided into six tenements and known anciently as "the Bull Inn". This inn does not at present seem picked up in other documents and is not mentioned by Beck (*Inns and Alehouses*). In September 1685 Robert Washington and Thomas Roberts, the latter expressly named in the deeds as one of the Bull Inn tenants, were presented by the manorial court "for suffering their travelling waggons to stand in the street in the night houre". They were to be amerced five shillings a year if this nuisance were not remedied. They would be warned again a year later (PHA 3955). The pair were clearly carriers by trade and it is probably this Robert Washington who is commemorated by the inset stone.

In 1700 Robert Payne a blacksmith is at the forge, and the smith's shop is mentioned again in 1718 when William Hunt and James Mills are in occupation. A barber and a blacksmith shared the corner site in 1721 while in 1753 the tenants were Thomas Waller perukemaker and Thomas Combs blacksmith (see WSRO MP 2573). Whether the forge was an integral part of the present Tudor Cottage premises is arguable. When George Combs the blacksmith died in 1808 he left his property to trustees and it was sold to Henry Upton of Petworth in the following year. A minute in the Churchwardens' Vestry Book for October 17th 1809 records that Mr. Tyler had reported to the Vestry that the Third Earl of Egremont "observing the dangerous state of the pitching in the Market Place, proposes that he will endeavour at his own expense, to purchase and pull down the blacksmith's shop and cottage at present projecting into the street or highway leading from the top of Pound Street toward the Market Place on the south side of the Swan Inn and by throwing the ground into the street to widen the same". The Vestry had in return to undertake certain drainage works; in particular constructing a four inch brick drain from the north east corner of the Market Square to the Lower Conduit. The Vestry accepted the proposal but no more is heard of it in CVB and no such truncation of the property appears in the deeds, on the other hand it is difficult to say now that the property projects into the street. Certainly if the corner were as narrow as the minute in CVB suggests then it is easy to see why Messrs. Washington and Roberts had caused such a nuisance with their waggons over a century before. Whatever the fate of the forge, the two premises that would be the baker's and the saddler's were sold to William Upton in 1809 and would remain in the Upton family until the death of Henry Upton in 1902.

In September 1902 the two properties were auctioned, along with the cottage and carpenter's shop in the alley adjoining the saddler's and other properties away to the west in Pound Street itself. The present Tudor Cottage is described as a Stationer's and Newspaper shop while "the other is, and has been for very many years, used as a Saddler's and Harness Maker's shop". Mr. Weeks the saddler was the overall tenant. The adjoining "brick and stone-built and tile-healed cottage" with carpenter's shop was in the occupation of Mr. John Tate as quarterly tenant. It is now the video shop in the alley. The census returns from 1841 consistently mention John Sumersell carpenter and it may be that this had been his workshop. It is however equally possible that Thomas Arnold, the long-established bootmaker, used these premises through the mid-nineteenth century. It is often difficult to establish precise locations with census returns.

Bill Ede vividly recalled working for John Tate in the 1920s (*Petworth Society Bulletin* No. 32) . . .

"From Mrs. Tiplady I went on to work for Mr. Tate in Saddlers Row. He was a busy man but most of his jobs turned out to be rather dusty ones. Basically I suppose he was an upholsterer and decorator but he also did undertaking. He would restuff mattresses — you would empty the mattress case, then put the contents (which had got hard and lumpy by this time) through what was called a "devil-killer", a drum with a set of fearsome spikes, something like a chaff-cutter. This would tear up the flock material and get rid of the lumps. You had to be careful or the thing would chop up your hand as well! And the dust! We didn't use the devil-killer on the Petworth House mattresses as these had coconut fibre in them and we had to sit down and pick it by hand before putting it back.

Another of Mr. Tate's jobs was carpet-beating. He would go out to the big houses at spring-cleaning time, take all the carpets outside, hang them on the line and beat them with a long stick. Mr. Tate certainly came up with some dusty jobs and if you had no blisters on your hands when you started you would certainly have a few when you'd finished. Picture-framing was another of his specialities but the undertaking I was never keen on and kept away from as much as I could. When he left the Swan Corner premises Mr. Tate moved up to High Street and I worked there with him for a time."

In the 1920s Messrs. Stevens the butcher's had the shop on the west side of the alley and there has been a butcher's there ever since. The shop on the corner does not seem to have been traditionally a commercial premises although Bill Ede could remember Mr. Lamboll, the carrier from the Pound, keeping some of his faggots and general stock in the big cellar there. He recalled when he was driving Mrs. Tiplady's trap that the lights were candles and that as he turned the Saddlers Row corner into Pound Street the wind caught the candles and blew them out. A policeman stopped him for driving without lights and Bill Ede asked him to feel the candle sockets which were still warm. The policeman let him go on to Mrs. Tiplady's stable at the Pound (*Petworth Society Bulletin* No. 32).

The one property other than the Swan on the northern side of the road is Bacon's the shoe shop. The property is without doubt age-old but its known history is patchy. No old name for it seems to exist and it is not marked on the 1882 Survey map. Some deeds, but possibly not all that are extant, form the group Add. MSS 35,555 to 35,571 at WSRO. The earliest of these dates from 1751 although there is passing mention of an older deed from 1604. In 1751 the property is described as "a messuage, backside and garden in Petworth, adjoining the tenement formerly of Wm. Young and now or late known by the name of the Swan" (35,555). The garden would presumably have stretched away northward along the line of the road. In the early nineteenth century James Challen, patten-maker, was here, no doubt using the premises as a shop. By 1862 the deeds describe them as "now or late in the occupation of William Dilloway" and Sophia Dilloway "dealer in meal" is mentioned here in the 1861 census. By the late century William Ovenden the tinsmith and stationer had moved down to the Saddlers Row corner from New Street and would remain there until Mr. Letchford moved down from Church Street in the exodus that resulted from the demolition of the houses in the churchyard. The shoe shop of course still continues. Bill Vincent (*Petworth Society Bulletin* No. 59) presents a vivid picture of working there evenings and Saturdays in the 1920s, delivering shoes, sweeping out the shop, helping to parcel up customers' shoes or using a rasp to make templates for the men working at the back repairing. The templates would guide them as they cut out the sides of leather to the size required for each individual repair. The men working in the small room at the back are the great difference between the 1920s and the present day. In the 1920s repairs were still executed on the premises and the muffled sound of the two repairers working at the back could still be heard in the shop itself.

# 15

## POUND STREET

POUND Street is so called because a cattle pound stood once on the Tillington Road corner. An older name is Sowter Street, but Pound Street could often simply be merged with its continuation Station Road and called "Mill Lane", the lane that led to Coultershaw Mill. Thomas Ederton's 1541 return is not informative on this street but Treswell's 1610 map clearly marks Sowter Street and shows it with more buildings on the west side than on the east, the reverse of the situation today. In Treswell's time Pound Street and Back Road formed a junction with West Street and Church Street, leading west into Petworth Park or east toward St. Mary's Church.

Memories of the Pound itself are dim now and fading fast: the remnants of it being pulled down in 1937. Motor traffic had already made it an anachronism. Henry Whitcomb who was born in the adjacent house recalls a large tank to water the animals and a high bank to the rear to prevent them escaping. The Pound had a high wall at the front too, high enough for Henry Whitcomb's brother to fall off at Goodwood time and concuss himself. He was picked up by some passing gypsies who looked in again after the races to see if he was alright. Obviously the very concept of a Pound presupposes little or no traffic. If someone had a stray they would report it to the police and the constable would in his turn tell the man who kept the Pound and lived in the little cottage at the side.

The problem of wandering livestock was by no means a new one: the manorial court never tired of castigating "those that suffer their hogges to go into the highway unringed and unyoked". In September 1684 the court decreed that "those whose hogs were found wandering would be amerced two shillings and sixpence for each one", but judging from their continued imprecations little action was taken. There was certainly a cattle pound in 1660; for the court, meeting in September of that year, presented "that there ought to be a stile on the west side of Petworth Pound goinge into the Field towards Rotherbridge" (PHA 3955). This would seem to imply much the same position as in later years. In 1662 Robert Tegrove and Francis Hayward were appointed "to drive all the hoggs that wander about the street to the Pound and that they shall have iiid for every hogg they do impound to be paid by the owner of the hogg" (PHA 3955).

On the face of it Pound Street is an unattractive street, like North Street receiving no relief from the one-way system and like North Street being pavemented on the one side only. This gives a somewhat unwelcoming impression. The pavement on the east side is in truth confined enough and many local people avoid Pound Street altogether because of the proximity of the traffic. Certainly as in North Street the roar and grime of passing vehicles does not encourage reflection. How often do visitors peer round the corner of Saddlers Row and stop as the long straight road leads apparently nowhere. Pound Street for the visitor leads out of the town rather than into it. The stream of cars may hurtle inexorably southward, but for the visiting pedestrian to venture down Pound Street is to risk falling off the globe altogether. Most take a quick look and turn back. Pound Street, almost as much as its continuation Park Road, keeps its own counsel. Its secrets, and secrets it most certainly has, are not for the casual visitor.

Culvercroft with its entrance on the western side of the street, opposite the junction with Saddlers Row, is one of Petworth's larger houses and is now divided. At the end of the nineteenth century it was for a time the residence of the manager of the old London and County Bank, ancestors of the present National Westminster, then home to Dr. Barnes, then Dr. Kerr. For a time it was used as a school and finally sold by the Leconfield Estate in the late 1960s. The name is certainly old; Treswell's map clearly showing an extensive area of over eight acres marked "Culver Crofte" extending west and north in the area of the present Petworth House Gardens and flanking the houses of West Street to the north. Culver of course is an old word for a dove. Jeffrey Hawkins, deposing before the Chancery in 1596 in the dispute between Henry the ninth Earl and his tenants over emparking, tells of a meeting between Henry Percy the eighth Earl and some sixteen of his tenants in the Culver Garden some twenty years previously. The Earl was seeking consent for a further emparking of common land to give his deer access from one park to another. The meeting had ended with a heated exchange between the Earl and Thomas Markes of Upperton, one of the more outspoken of his tenants. Encountering spirited resistance to his proposal, the Earl had departed with the words, "Markes, Markes, I will be even with thee". It would seem that the site of the Culver Garden should be located in this approximate area (*Cloakbag and Common Purse* p. 28). The present Culvercroft is a successor to an earlier large house owned at the time of the 1762 Window Tax Return by Thomas Elder, sometime steward to Charles, Duke of Somerset. The high wall flanking Pound Street is popularly supposed to have been built by French prisoners of war in the Napoleonic times but, persistent as the tradition is, I have never found any trace of evidence to corroborate it.

The House in Pound Street is long and narrow, having almost all its rooms to the front. Formerly, tradition has it, it was a dairy, but for generations it was home to the Whitcomb family, so many of whom worked for the Leconfield Estate. The name is new but the house itself may in some form go back as far as the seventeenth century. Magnolia on the bank is traditionally the Leconfield Estate forester's house, Mr. Wilcox being there between the wars. The lay-by marks the site of old cottages pulled down in the 1950s. Pound Street was less open then, the cottages, hugging the road, giving a much more enclosed feel then than now. The enclosed nuttery to the south is one of the least known corners of Petworth and the high wall still carries beneath its blowing ivy traces of the gun-ports cut out in 1940 to give protection and a field of fire, up and down the road, in case of invasion. Looking back fifty years later there seems almost an echo of the Napoleonic wars about such provisions. There were similar positions in North Street. Slightly further down and in line with York Cottage concrete pits two and a half feet deep were excavated, a foot square at the top. To allow traffic to pass these holes were filled with removable concrete slabs. In the event of attack these slabs would be removed and angular pieces of steel inserted. In theory these would prevent the passage of motorised vehicles such as tanks and armoured cars (see J. Taylor in *Petworth Society Bulletin* No. 39).

Cockthrowing was of old time a staple recreation on the

Tillington Road corner says the nineteenth century author of the Tales of Old Petworth. It was a pastime he considered quite debased in comparison with cock-fighting "a very different quality of sport from cock-throwing — or a man of brains shying at a helpless, brainless cock". Regarding cock-throwing, Arnold, writing in 1864, agrees: after talking of the obsolete custom of bull-baiting he continues, "throwing at cocks on Shrove Tuesday was another practice no less demoralizing. These birds are said to have been trained to avoid the staff thrown at them, by adroitly jumping or flying away. If struck so that the legs were broken or the poor biped was stunned, and did not recover before a certain time, it became the property of the striker. This debasing pastime was carried on at the corner of the road which leads to Tillington". (*History* pp. 90-1.) It may be doubted however whether Arnold shared his contemporary's rather charitable view of cock-fighting.

Newlands, built for a Dr. Newlands in the eighteenth century and one of Petworth's classic gentry houses, returned 27 windows in the 1762 assessment. Much of the large garden to the rear has been taken for car parking and the house itself is now an outpost garrison for the local council. Early century photographs show the house with extensive greenhouses attached to the southern side, and there are photographs too of the interior of the house at this period.

York Cottage is that comparative rarity, a true three storey house: it has also an extensive cellar. Nairn speaks of it as having a north of England air about it. Arthur Allison, water foreman to the Leconfield Estate, called it York Cottage in the late 1920s after Yorkshire where he had been born and had worked for the Leconfield Estate before coming to Petworth in 1888. He was still working in 1951 when he died. The men would line up along the brick garden path outside the kitchen window to be paid. Campanula ran right along the border edge and there were hydrangeas against the brick wall of Newlands. I expect a similar weekly wages ceremony was enacted by Mr. Wilcox at Magnolia. Pound Street, like North Street, while it has always had private houses, had something of the character of a Leconfield Estate enclave. York Cottage, curiously, was not an Estate property, Mr. Allison having bought it privately, a most unusual action for an Estate servant at that time.

Pound Street looking south 1934. A pencil drawing by Charles Leazell.

We have spoken of Pound Street as holding its secrets, and No. 22, unobtrusive as it seems, certainly does so. What relation the number 22 has to the other houses in the street is one secret, but the title deeds have a larger one. 22 Pound Street was in the early eighteenth century a meeting-house for the Presbyterian cause and a good part of the present house was constructed as such. A legacy of those days are the rounded window alcoves on the south side, now part of the outside wall. No one who looks at them can doubt that they were built for a place of worship.

Under the Commonwealth the Presbyterian cause had been dominant in Petworth, as elsewhere, and Francis Cheynell, a zealous partisan of the Presbyterian cause, had replaced Henry King as Rector of Petworth. King would be reinstated in 1660. When the Church of England was re-established at the Restoration, all ministers were required to conform or be ejected from their living. As some, despite ejection, continued to preach, the draconian Conventicle Act of 1664 was brought in, effectively prohibiting public demonstrations of worship by dissenters. The Five Mile Act of 1665 levied huge fines on any non-conforming minister venturing within five miles of his previous living. The 1670 Conventicle Act was slightly less severe but offered large inducements to informers. A conventicle of some fifty to sixty persons is recorded at Petworth in 1669 and the practising ministers are known Presbyterians. It is probable that clandestine meetings were held at Byworth to make them less vulnerable to informers and that the Presbyterians continued to meet there even after the Toleration Act in the early 1690s restored a measure of religious freedom. Certainly the Presbyterians are at Byworth in 1707. Thomas Hallett, expelled from Streat in East Sussex in 1672, was in the Petworth area until his death in 1707 while John Buckley was minister from 1714-1720. Grants made by the Presbyterian Fund of London to help congregations maintain their ministers show this clearly.

In 1724 the title deeds of 22 Pound Street speak of a plot of land some 39 by 29 feet, part of the garden of an existing house, "on which is now erecting and almost erected an edifice at the cost of Edward Madgwick of Tillington Esq. and John Aylwin of Petworth gent." The messuage formerly in the possession of William

Honyman stood near the Pound, adjoining a tenement and garden in the occupation of William Sayres to the north, the highway from the town of Petworth to the west and a tenement and garden in the occupation of Samuel Anchor to the south. A conveyance in trust follows dated 27th November 1725. Jeremiah Owen is the minister and responsible for both Petworth and Thakeham, grant being made for him by the Presbyterian Fund for the years 1722-1726. He left for Barnet in 1726 and no minister is known after that. The next deed from March 1790 speaks of "a freehold edifice commonly called and for some years since used as a meeting-house for Presbyterians but for many years last past disused, deserted and totally neglected". The chapel windows remained but the Meeting House itself was totally forgotten. The congregation seems to have shared in the general Presbyterian decline in the mid-eighteenth century, due in considerable part to the embracing by some ministers and some lay people of an Arian theology. (For this see Neil Caplan: *Protestant dissent in Petworth* in *Petworth Society Magazine* No. 60 and for an abstract of the deeds of No. 22 WSRO MP 2361.)

There adjoin smaller cottages, one at least of considerable antiquity with timber framing that has attracted artists and photographers over the years. All have small intimate gardens to the rear hemmed in by a high stone wall. Box Grove, the next house, is apparently so called after the box hedge that extends for much of the pavemented side of Pound Street. By tradition it is the box hedge seen by Cobbett in August 1823 "just as I came out of Petworth, more than twelve feet broad and about fifteen feet high. I dare say it is several centuries old. I think it is about forty yards long. It is a great curiosity". The hedge, one would suppose, has suffered from decades of traffic fumes but, particularly if it be Cobbett's hedge, from the passage of time. The bowed trunks certainly bespeak a long sojourn there but whether the hedge has been replanted since Cobbett's time is hard now to say: he obviously thought the hedge venerable even in his time. At certain seasons the minuscule leaves blow up and down the street and into every cranny, often forming small solid off-green eddies held together by cobwebs.

At the turn of the present century Box Grove was home to the Brydone family but, of its history prior to that, little is known. There may well be nineteenth century connections with the well-known Petar family. Old the house certainly is. Before the Great War, and continuing through and after, the Misses Austin ran one of the old-fashioned private schools that could still flourish in those days: a shade more refined perhaps than the ordinary day school. The garden has only recently fallen victim to the insatiable demand for car-parking space. One of Petworth's ancient gardens bartered for thirty parking places. It is a dilemma that endures. Petworth's great beauty lies in its hidden gardens and their erosion erodes Petworth itself. The last large apple tree could be seen literally being torn apart by a JCB, the latter almost sentient in its insistent crunching menace and the whole seeming like a ritual execution. Once there had been a monkey-puzzle tree but that had long gone. Croquet had been played on the lawn and the schoolchildren nipped at the eschscholzia bonnets. Mercifully Cobbett's chance recollection of the hedge should protect it from future predatory JCBs. The children would play in and out of the double row of bushes and the Misses Austin would walk down the central path in the cool of the day. Curiously the hedge is not deemed suitable for a formal tree preservation order. "A hedge is not a tree" being the received wisdom as I understand it. Appropriately enough in later years, the Misses Austin retired to another Boxgrove, this time the village near Chichester.

Trowels, far away on the further side of the box hedge is old property too, the roof timbers showing the characteristic smoke-blackening that bespeaks great age. John Philp's inventory of 1688 (WSRO Ep 1/29) can be confidently linked with Trowels and suggests that he had virtually given up the trade of bricklayer stated on his inventory and taken a new calling of publican. Indeed as Miss Beck suggests (*Inns and Alehouses* p. 143) he seems to have named his new pub after his old calling. The cellar contained in 1688 seven kilderkins full of strong beer worth in all two pounds nine shillings. A fair quantity this: a kilderkin holding 16 to 18 gallons. John Philp had also in the cellar a regular armoury of other brewing equipment, not simply more, no doubt empty, kilderkins, but barrels, hogsheads, brewing tubs, covers, water tubs and a hundredweight of hops. The cellar may have been a little congested for Philp had also crammed in a load of coal, a hundred faggots, three cord of wood, two ladders and a miscellany of tools! The house is described as the Trowell in an Estate receipt book of 1696 (Beck ibid) and it is likely that it is Trowels that is referred to by the manorial court in 1682 as "John Philp's mansion house" (PHA 3955). Somewhat oddly for a mansion house, Philp's hogpen and privy were causing a public nuisance!

While it is unusual to have a probate inventory such as John Philp's which is tied to a particular identifiable house as this one seems to be, it is very difficult in practice to tie in the rooms in the inventory with those in the present house. In addition to the cellar, a kitchen is mentioned, a hall, a little room next to the kitchen, a chamber over the hall, a next chamber and a room over the passage. The public house was defunct by 1756, although the name Trowel has survived, and the house clearly reverted to private use. The present shop premises appear to have been added later. In 1885 the premises saw service as a temporary Post Office while the Market Square premises were undergoing repair, while for the next three decades they housed a shoe shop, first Wagstaff and Sons, then Bennetts. A memory survives of Mr. Bennett going out to Graffham, as doubtless he did to other villages, to take orders from working men who wanted strong boots. He would make them and bring them out on his next journey. The shop has been a greengrocers for some seventy years. One last thought: Arnold's *History* (p. 89) mentions an unidentified pub called the Brick and Mortar as existing during the reign of Queen Anne. Might this just have been a later variation on Philp's original sign of the Trowel? Unlikely I suppose, but just possible.

The present fish shop next to Trowels has been a commercial premises as long as photographs can show but this does not take us back beyond the 1890s, no really old picture of Pound Street being known to survive. In fact it was still a private house when sold with other property in adjoining Saddlers Row in September 1902. Mr. Payne set up as a butcher just before the 1914 war and when he moved to East Street the shop continued as a butchers, Messrs. Joyes selling fish as well as meat in the 1920s. Melicent Knight recalls the Petworth butchers meeting as a committee during the 1914-1918 war in the front room (now the restaurant) of the present fish shop to plan the allocation of meat to each butcher. "It wasn't a straightforward decision, but had to be apportioned according to the proportion of the total trade each butcher enjoyed, i.e. the butcher who did the biggest trade had also the largest allocation of meat". She remembers them seated amicably round a table at their deliberations (*Petworth Society Bulletin* No. 51).

Pound Place to the rear of the fish shop is a small cul-de-sac with two characterful houses, the further one, Quoins, appearing the younger of the two. While considerably renovated the more westerly house seems to have medieval origins. Pound Place was anciently known as Gosden's Yard and the name appears occasionally in old documents. It is one of those popular names that, lacking the buttress of official day to day use, are on the verge of being lost completely. Probably Gosden's Yard is already beyond recall, for its use would now be a conscious, and for most, a bewildering, anachronism. The name is certainly old, Joseph Gosden returning seven windows in the 1762 Window Tax Assessment. He appears to have been a builder and almost certainly occupied the right-hand and older of the two houses in Pound Place. Dockets found in the house during restoration work in the early 1970s show another builder William Pulling (or Pullen) in possession in the 1820s and indeed the Pulling family can through these dockets be traced, with long gaps, through to the 1870s. The documents are strictly business; a few estimates, various invoices, some lists of hours worked and wages paid. Mr. Pulling employed several men. Perhaps the most interesting are receipts for school fees for the Pulling children in the years up to 1842, James Woodcock and Elizabeth Joyes running separate private establishments for boys and girls respectively.

The present Good Will premises were occupied in the early century by Messrs. Golds butchers and fishmongers. For many years Miss Fanny Knight ran a small sweet shop on the premises, rather like Mrs. Palmer's at the foot of High Street. Mrs. Palmer gaining at one time an advantage by managing to supply her youthful clientele with hot drinks. Under later proprietors the trade broadened its base into general grocery, the shop finally succumbing as a grocery store in the early 1980s.

Bill Vincent recalls Pound Place and Pound Street just after the Great War (*Petworth Society Magazine* No. 59).

POUND STREET

The circus comes to town! Pound Street September 1958. The elephants have come up from Petworth Station. *Photograph by George Garland. Garland Collection.*

"Pound Place wasn't called Pound Place when I first lived there during the 1914-18 war: it was just Pound Street, although some people called it Gosden's Yard, an old name which has just about died out. There wasn't much traffic about in those days so that I could just wander out of the yard and into Pound Street itself. Fanny Knight's sweetshop was on the right and what odd pennies I had I'd spend in there. It was very dim inside the shop and it always seemed an age before the old lady came in. No bags then: the sweets would be weighed out and then Fanny Knight would roll a sheet of paper into a cone, put the sweets in and then turn in the top of the cone. Sweets were always loose then and I remember she always had broken chocolate for sale as other shops had broken biscuits. On the other side of the alley was Mr. Payne's the butchers but as a small boy of course I didn't go into the butchers as I would the sweetshop. I can still see the huge blocks of ice that were delivered and left on the Pound Street pavement. They would be hauled into the butchers with large metal tongs and put into the ice room. Just down the road was West's fruit and vegetable shop and next to that Mr. Todman the piano-tuner's shop. It was often closed because he was out tuning pianos but I was always fascinated by the small display of musical instruments he had in the window, a banjo, a flute or two, a clarinet perhaps. I recall him coming to tune our piano; he had a little Gladstone bag with his tools and he'd take quite a long time lifting the front off, then the back and tightening the strings. After a while Mr. Todman gave up the shop and just went out from his home in East Street."

Pound Street today is something of a chameleon, quiet during the day except for the steady stream of traffic but springing to vicarious life at night when the two food establishments ply their trade. Few if any of those who pull up on the pavement, jump out and reappear with their purchases in plastic carrier or paper bag give a thought to William Cobbett riding by, Jeremiah Owen and his Presbyterian congregation or even John Philp's anti-social hog-pen. Pound Street has its secrets and it holds them close.

# 16

## STATION ROAD

PETWORTH residents of a couple of centuries ago would no doubt consider this book somewhat perverse: difficult enough to traverse the muddy, rutted roads without celebrating them in a book. Doubly perverse perhaps to dignify what is now Station Road as a street. Mill Lane, as they knew it, was simply a long cul-de-sac leading to the Mill at Coultershaw and had been such for generations. The main road from the south branched off at Kilsham Lane, traversed the Rother at Rotherbridge and went off up Hungers Lane. Heavy going indeed! The road over Coultershaw would not be made until the early nineteenth century.

Station Road owes its name of course to the station built two miles out of town and two miles out of Lord Leconfield's sight and in the great days of railway travel it would be Station Road that afforded the visitor a first view of Petworth. Alighting from the "Petworth flyer" at the station the travellers would be met by the horse bus that plied between Petworth Station and Market Square and met all trains. Arrivals could have an element of the austere, Mrs. Greest in *Petworth Society Bulletin* No. 24 vividly recalling her first minutes at Petworth in the early 1920s coming to Petworth House to work as a housemaid.

> "The housekeeper at Petworth had given me detailed instructions about coming from my home in Derbyshire, down in the train to Kings Cross, then by taxi across unknown London to Victoria. I had the exact time of the train to Pulborough, where I had to change to go along the branch line to Petworth, watching at each of the little stations to see which would be Petworth. There I would be met. And so I came to Petworth — just a name to me then: the other travellers alighted and disappeared, the train moved off and I was left alone. After about five minutes a horse-drawn carriage pulled up and a voice said, "Are you the new housemaid for Petworth House?"

I would know the driver later as Bill Barnes. We set off for Petworth House up the slight hill from the station and into the old town".

Petworth House staff might dispense with the station bus which was effectively an institution in itself. E. V. Lucas writing at the turn of the century knew it well and his phrase "one of those long close prisons that annihilate thought by their shattering unfixedness" sticks in the mind although I am never quite sure what he meant by it. The best description of the bus is probably this article from the *West Sussex Gazette* (March 1919).

### THE 7 GENTLEMEN OF PETWORTH AND THE LADY ON THE TOP OF THE 'BUS

Lady wishes to thank the 7 gentlemen who kept the inside of the Petworth omnibus warm on Friday while she rode outside in the teeth of a gale.

She trusts that the unavoidable rigours of the journey have in no case resulted in a chill.

This advertisement appeared in the Agony column of the *West Sussex Gazette*.

Eager to discover whether the Chesterfieldian manners of Petworth had gone to the dogs I went down to this little Sussex town of 1,500 inhabitants.

I climbed to a seat in a two-horsed 'bus beside the driver, and found he had much to say about the lady and the seven gentlemen.

"If she grumbles about riding outside once," he said, "what about me doing it for 17 years, and in all weathers? As a matter of fact, she could have had a seat inside had she liked. One of the gentlemen was quite willing to go outside, but she did not seem very eager to take the opportunity."

### DIVIDED CAMP.

Petworth, I found, was full of the incident. About half of the inhabitants sided with the lady, the others taking opposite views.

Mr. John Pitfield, the town's leading solicitor, who was one of the seven, corroborated the driver's story. "It was the 'bus for the three o'clock train," he said, "and we started from Petworth about 2.40."

"I was the last man to enter the 'bus; there was a lady inside and

STATION ROAD

Horse bus turning into Saddlers Row, 1897. (Queen Victoria's Diamond Jubilee). From a lantern-slide.

about six men. I did not see any other passengers inside and I got in and sat hard on Joe Vine, the Sussex cricketer. I heard afterward that there were some people waiting to get in, including a lady, and as it was starting to rain I offered to get out.

"The driver, however, said that a fly would follow, and I assumed that the lady was coming in it. I was surprised when we got to the station to see her descend from the 'bus.

"There was no gale, but there was unpleasant drizzle, and the feathers on her hat were a bit damp.

"I am sure no discourtesy was intended. Any of us would willingly have gone outside had we known."

Meantime great readiness has been shown on the part of the men of Petworth to ride outside the 'bus this week.

The station had been built when the railway came through in 1859 and, for a brief while until the line to Midhurst was completed, Petworth was the terminus, being honoured of course with the turntable. It was the prospect of trade generated by the railway that led to the building of the Railway Inn, afterward the Racehorse and more recently the Badger and Honeyjar. An older station of polished deal seems to have been demolished in the late 1880s to be replaced with the present single storey wooden structure, now converted into a private house. The new building had been formally opened by the Duke of Connaught staying at Petworth House at the time as member of a shooting party. The Prince of Wales would come to Petworth Station on a similar shooting trip in 1899. Passenger services survived until 1955, freight services not succumbing until 1966.

While the station was, in historic terms, relatively new, milling at nearby Coultershaw had a tradition going back hundreds of years. The old Coultershaw Mill was destroyed by fire in April 1923 and replaced by a more pragmatic construction of cement and steel in the American tradition. The demolition of this new mill in the early 1970s finally brought milling at Coultershaw to an end. The mill-stones of old Coultershaw were turned by a paddled waterwheel with the water coming onto the wheel being controlled by a flood gate. A shaft from the water wheel went through the bottom floor of the mill and from this shaft different size pulleys took belts up through the different machines on the three floors of the mill.

Lighting was with primitive candlesticks — just pieces of wood with three nails holding the candle. The spilt grease made the floors slippery. A candle was used too as lighting when the outside flood-gates were pulled up at night, a somewhat hazardous operation at the best of times. In the last years of the old mill a dynamo was run off the wheel and this dispensed, to a considerable extent, with the candles. Basic equipment was kept on the higher floor because the ground floor particularly was subject to periodical flooding. Ern. Hollingdale who worked at the old mill recalled how "the water would rise to one foot or eighteen inches all over the ground floor and the water-rats would take over. They were huge and completely unafraid and would just sit there and defy anyone to make them move. They always went off when the water subsided". By the flood gates was a brick built eel-trap with iron bars and a small gate. After a thunderstorm there might be half a hundred-weight or more of eels in there.

The great fire of 1923 would be talked about for years, the Hollingdale family at Heath End, workers at the mill for generations, being woken in the middle of the night with the news that the mill was on fire. The man on the split weekend shift had left at midnight on the Saturday to return at midnight on the Sunday. Bert. Hollingdale remembered crossing the bridge and having to crook his arm across his face to protect himself from the intense heat. The mill itself was already well alight. Petworth Fire Brigade arrived with their manual pump and directed their attention to preventing the spread of the fire, dousing the stables and sheds with water, the mill being past salvation. Petworth House Fire Brigade arrived later, their steam fire engine being towed down from Petworth House with Mr. Crawley desperately at work getting up a head of steam at the rear. As day began to break the Midhurst Fire Brigade arrived with their motor-driven engine and resplendent in their new brass helmets. They were at this time perhaps as much a boost to morale as an aid to fire-fighting. Someone dispatched to Henry Streeter at the Railway Inn to find refreshment received the immortal reply: "Yes, there's bread and cheese and something to drink, but if you'd told me you were coming I'd have got something prepared".

George Garland's early years had been spent at the Railway Inn, his widowed mother having married Henry Streeter the landlord. His friendship with Brother Lawrence, a Franciscan from the little community just up the road at Duncton, gave him an interest in photography which never left him. He would be Petworth's photographer for nearly half a century. Early prints were washed in the old stone trough outside the Railway Inn and the first pictures he sold to the national press were of a paint lorry that had skidded over the parapet at Coultershaw in January 1922. The fields to either side of the road into Petworth are the very heartland of his early photographs and his work has immortalised a time-honoured way of farming that would soon be swept away for ever. Garland's early work abounds with shots of horses working at Coultershaw, Hoes, Soanes and Frog, and the carters that worked with them live again in his pictures. Some fields remain as fields but the more northerly, nearest Petworth, have been taken over for housing. Elgar lived briefly at Hoes, away to the east with his daughter Mrs. Blake before moving to Brinkwells at Bedham. A youthful Henry Whitcomb was once stopped by the great man, Elgar claiming that the way past Hoes was private, Henry Whitcomb politely dissenting. The hunting bridge at the end of the lane was open to those who fished the Rother. Elgar protested, Henry Whitcomb stood his ground and the two parted amicably enough. It was only later that Henry Whitcomb divined that the slightly-built grey-haired stranger had been the famous composer.

As the road bends there are the outpost cottages of Stoney Hill, the wind it seems forever challenging and questioning their presence in his domain. At the crossroads a track leads west to Rotherbridge on the river, while to the east the ancient settlement of Haslingbourne lies in the dip. Holding one's course for Petworth however, fields again intervene before the new housing estates, but the station horse-bus would have passed only the Gasworks on the left, the two gasworks cottages on the hill opposite and the southern lodge of Littlecote House. The Gasworks were demolished in 1963 but the site remains and is still used by Southern Gas. The old building had the date of construction 1836 embossed on the front — the year before Queen Victoria's accession. The Gas Company in its earlier days was a very "Petworth" concern, shares being bought by those locally who could afford them — a somewhat restricted

Harold Kitchener at work at Petworth Gasworks March 1950. *Photograph by George Garland. Garland Collection.*

franchise one suspects. The works would have originally been sited as far out of Petworth as practicable, rather as in earlier times the tanneries had been. Coke could be bought there and the old men of the town would congregate in winter for a warm and a chat. One school of thought considered the coke fumes helpful in warding off diphtheria and one of the Petworth doctors would regularly bring his children down to inhale them. It was from here that Dickie Carver the lamplighter would set off on his regular and punctual round of the Petworth gas-lamps. When the older people claimed they could set their clocks by him it was no idle boast.

The first council houses, called Lloyd George Cottages, were put up just before the Great War, the rent of five shillings a week seeming somewhat stiff compared with Leconfield rents. The old name appears soon to have been discarded. Florie Pugh, whose parents were the first to move in, was told that for the first few weeks after April 1914 they lived there with eleven unfinished houses alongside. Station Road still retained its primeval quietness: she recalls, "We never saw air planes or motor cars, in fact Station Road was our playground, we'd be out playing in the road all day with a ball, or hoop and stick, or a pair of home-made stilts, or a bit of Mum's clothes line for a skipping rope . . ."

The north lodge of Littlecote House is perhaps a little earlier than Lloyd George cottages and was built by Whitcombs the Grove Street builders, the construction being particularly remembered for an incident when Jig Hill, in later years Petworth's roadmender, fell from a scaffold and injured his back. There was a long drive leading to Littlecote House, in latter years home to the agent of the Leconfield Estate. The present Littlecote Estate of course recalls the big house. Another addition, this time from the mid-1920s, is the wooden shed-like structure now used by an electrical contractor but for nearly two generations George Garland's photographic studio.

In more leisured times than these it was the custom on Sunday evenings to walk down to the Studio to see what had been put on display in the Garland showcases there — a local wedding perhaps or some local event, but even at this time Station Road was losing its old quiet and the absence of a pavement could lead to a certain unease. The Studio was the base for George Garland's frequent expeditions abroad to find country pictures to sell to the national press on a freelance basis. He sought particularly scenes or characters that would evoke, for a largely urbanised readership, a half-forgotten pastoral world that they were sure still survived if only they had the leisure and opportunity to rediscover it. Above all they needed the reassurance that this world still existed and it was George Garland's livelihood to go out and find this world for them, or at least some approximation to it. Mrs. Garland would remain at the Studio printing or dealing with the other day to day minutiae of the business. Charles White, later photographer at Midhurst, who worked at the Studio for a time in the early 1930s, recalled those days vividly. George Garland would return often quite late from a day in the country "and the staff would know roughly what kind of day he had had by the door he came in at — if it had been good he came through the side door, if bad by the front door — perhaps with a quick kick at the old suitcases full of spare prints which stood at one side!"

The Station Road allotments on the east side were entered through where the fire-station is now, there being a meadow fronting on the road known of old as Howard's Plat because the Howard brothers, the Petworth sweeps, used to let out ponies and carts for hire from here — the field being rented from the Leconfield Estate. Before 1914 it was used as an occasional venue for travelling theatres of a type not likely to gain Lord Leconfield's approval to use the Town Hall or Iron Room — or if the truth be known, to seek it! Henry Whitcomb remembers one particular company which rejoiced in the name of Taylor's Gaff. The name in itself had a somewhat exotic air and detracted nothing from the atmosphere; few in the audience would know that Gaff is a slang name for a cheap or disreputable music hall or theatre. Taylor's Gaff would stay for about a week and bring stage, curtains and marquee by horse and cart, siting their living waggons in the meadow. Henry Whitcomb found a play about the Red Barn murders so enthralling that he stayed for two consecutive performances having crawled in unofficially under the awning to start with! Bill Ede recalled marionnette players, a man and his wife lodging with the Ede family in High Street before the Great War. They had some kind of tented cover and would put on a show for the children on Howard's Plat.

The orchard and allotment land to the north and east of Howard's Plat had formerly been cornfields but when this did not give the landlord a sufficient return it was, in 1868, let out to individual tenants for growing fruit and vegetables. The large plots thus provided gave an annual rental of some £35. The orchard and allotment land would appear to have extended through to the road where the two houses now lie between the Pound Garage and the new Fire Station but no photograph of this is known to survive. James Groom, correspondent of *The Garden* magazine, came to Petworth from his home in Gosport in the late August of 1885 expressly to see William Jacob's fruit trees and saw, fronting on to Station Road and extending away to the east, the finest display of apples he had ever seen. Jacob's orchard had all the best old varieties such as Scarlet Nonpareil, Melon Apple and others but Groom had come particularly to see William Jacob's stock of his new introduction Lady Sudeley, formerly known as Jacob's Strawberry.

William Jacob was an altogether unusual man: born at Lyminge in Kent in 1819 he was not only a horticulturist of note but a Methodist lay preacher and a practised taxidermist. As a young man he had worked for some years on a fruit farm at Sharsted near Chatham as a farm bailiff and while at Sharsted he sems to have discovered the apple that years later would be named Lady Sudeley; whether as a chance seedling or by deliberate experiment is not known. Nor is it known why Jacob should have come to Petworth, or where he kept his precious original stock when he first arrived. In 1861 he was living in New Street and is described in the census of that year as a "sheep doctor". It was not until 1868 that he was able to plant up the orchard that would later become known as Jacob's Orchard, a term surviving orally well into the present century. It would be some years again before William Jacob could establish himself as a grower of prize-winning fruit and find at long last official recognition for his new apple. James Groom had described the Lady Sudeley in 1884 as "beautifully striped with carmine on a yellow ground . . . traces of russet on it bespeak good quality". Groom thought its fruiting season of late August an important feature commercially "for the simple reason that foreign competition does not set in with any great force until the American barrels arrive" (*The Garden* 27th September 1884).

Demolition of Coultershaw Mill about 1970. *Photograph by George Garland. Garland Collection.*

Station Road then is the adoptive home of the Lady Sudeley: the name being changed from Jacob's Strawberry in deference to the owner of the largest fruit farm in the country at that time. Over the years the memory of William Jacob faded but many of the trees of his planting remained. Miss Maggie Wootton claimed that she had an apple tree on her back lawn next to the Pound Garage which had been the original Lady Sudeley. With William Jacob long forgotten, the information meant little enough, but, given our greater awareness now of William Jacob, the tradition looks to be correct. Where else might one seek the original Lady Sudeley? Gwenda Morgan could remember the ancient tree blowing down and the rather forlorn remains being sawn up and taken away. The tree would have been well over a century old. While Jacob's Orchard was probably dismembered by the building of the two houses next to the Pound Garage in the 1920s, some of the original trees were clearly left in the ample gardens. The land to the rear was not developed until the late 1950s, much of it remaining as allotment up to that time but much too as ageing orchard, the trees spindly and lichened but still bearing fruit of all kinds including of course Lady Sudeley apples, the orchard floor in spring being a riot of forget-me-not and naturalised tulips.

The site of the present Empire Garage had simply a large barn standing on it backing on to the allotment land. It was a base for William Lamboll the Petworth carrier, but with the coming of the motor car would assume a somewhat busier aspect, profiting no doubt from its position at the junction of important roads. Part of the large site was made over to Mr. George Knight's car-repairing business and Cleveland petrol was sold at tenpence halfpenny a gallon. For a time Petworth's cinema was here. Vic Roberts, the Guildford carrier, had the site in the early 1920s, renting out part as garages and using the rest as a base. His business was to ply between Petworth and Guildford, leaving Mondays and Thursdays and returning Tuesdays and Fridays. The carrier would go round the Petworth shops on the Monday and Thursday morning taking their orders before setting off, calling also at the more well-to-do private houses. As the 1920s advanced orders might come in by telephone. Once in Guildford he would put up at the Lion and Crown in North Street. Bert Exall who worked with him as a lad recalled that it was not unusual to take hens that hadn't laid properly to sell at Guildford Market and find that, what with the bumping of the solid tyres of the lorry and the shaking of the frame at the top, the reluctant hens had performed their duty. The landlady at the Lion and Crown would cook them the eggs for breakfast. Many of the Petworth tradesmen had already bought their goods, simply wanting Mr. Roberts to bring them back. There might be a side of beef for the butcher perhaps, the meat covered in sacking and kept cool by huge blocks of ice carried on the iron rack on the top. The blocks of ice would be sold also to the Petworth butchers as an aid to refrigeration. Bananas, another staple item, might, one supposes, be less tolerant of the dripping ice!

Station Road, alias Mill Lane, is in a way a newcomer to Petworth's street system. It was the time-honoured track to the Mill yet it seems too almost a parvenu. It does not have the buildings of character that enable some Petworth streets to retain an identity of their own despite the depredations of the traffic. In a way perhaps it is the originally unspoiled character of Station Road that has left it so defenceless. Few, one suspects, of those who drive through on the way south give Station Road much thought. Here to the superficial eye is just one more short piece of semi-urban sprawl on the edge of an historic town, one more thirty mile per hour zone to chafe at or flout at one's peril. We may leave the last word with Florie Pugh (*Petworth Society Bulletin* No. 36:

> "How it has all changed! The cornfield on the west side has made way for a large housing estate, and the same on the east side which was all orchards and so beautiful in springtime when they were all abloom. My playground, the road, is alive with traffic rushing up and down all day and half the night, but that's progress and we all have to go with the times!"